They Called Him JOE

An Extraordinary Story of an Ordinary Man

They Called Him Joe

Al Long and Tad Long

ISBN 1-929478-62-3 (softcover)

Cross Training Publishing
317 West Second Street
Grand Island, NE 68801
(308) 384-5762

Copyright © 2003 by Cross Training Publishing

All rights reserved. No part of this book may be reproduced without written permission from the publisher, except by a reviewer who may quote brief passages in a review; nor may any part of this book be reproduced, stored in a retrieval system or transmitted in any form or other without written permission from the publisher.

This book is manufactured in the United States of America.

Library of Congress Cataloging in Publication Data in Progress.

Published by Cross Training Publishing,
317 West Second Street
Grand Island, NE 68801

Disclaimer

The authors of this book would like to acknowledge that there may be errors of omission and fact in this document. It is the best faith effort on the authors' part to give a true and accurate account of Reverend George Huff's life. Please accept that these are human authors trying to portray a man of God's life the way we were led.

All Scripture references are in NIV unless otherwise indicated.

DEDICATION

This book is dedicated to Edna Huff. Her life, along with many others, shaped who Joe was and therefore impacted countless other lives.

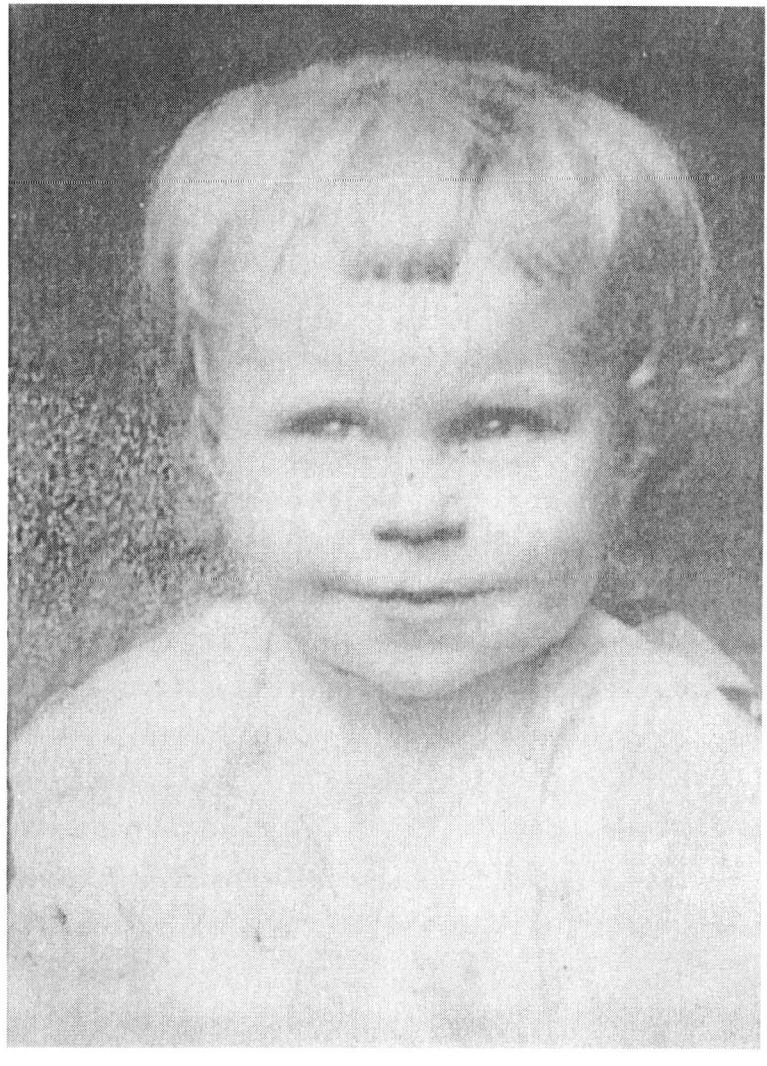

Acknowledgement

Many people are to thank for their input and help in this adventure. Most especially, we thank Carol (Huff) Long for all her insight, wisdom and council throughout this journey as well as her direct input into the content and editing.

Special Thanks Goes To the Family of Joe

Mary Huff, wife; Charlotte (Huff) Walker, sister; George W. Huff, Jr. (Billy), son; and Betty Huff-Long, daughter. Without their collective input, the account of Joe's life would not have been as detailed, nor complete.

PROLOGUE

It was a dark and dreary late winter day in Central Indiana. Joe had been in the nursing home for nearly two months, much longer than anyone expected. When he was admitted, no one thought he would live that long. That was typical of Joe, though. He always did the unexpected.

The disease had taken away his personality, his ability to speak and communicate, but not his desire to live. To the very end Joe fought the battle to stay alive much like he had lived his own life, with every ounce of courage he could muster. This was a bit puzzling to some because they all knew where he would be going, to spend eternity with his heavenly father. Still the human side of Joe still fought to stay on this earth to serve as long as he possibly could. The physical body fought to stay alive, while the spirit was ready to enter a place of peace.

Many had been with Joe all through his nursing home experience. His wife of over 50 years was there as well as friends, family and people from his church. On the last day of Joe's life he was with many of those same individuals. Because it was evident to all that the end was near, Joe was moved to a private room where he could spend the last hours of his life with his loved ones.

It became increasingly evident that Joe was losing the physical battle and there would be no more delaying the end. As he breathed the last breath of his earthly existence his mind must have raced back over the years now past, all the experiences that had shaped him and the influence he had on those who had been a part of his long and productive journey.

As a single tear streamed down his now sunken cheek, something happened—a brief smile seemed to appear on his lips. Then everything became still.

Seven Ages of Man

All the world's a stage,
And all the men and women merely players:
They have their exits and their entrances;
And one man in his time plays many parts,
His acts being seven ages. At first the infant,
Mewling and puking in the nurse's arms.
And then the whining school-boy, with his satchel,
And shining morning face, creeping like snail
Unwilling to school. And then the lover,
Sighing like furnace, with a woeful ballad
Made to his mistress' eyebrow. Then a soldier,
Full of strange oaths, and bearded like the pard,
Jealous in honor, sudden and quick in quarrel,
Seeking the bubble reputation
Even in the cannon's mouth. And then the justice,
In fair round belly with good capon lined,
With eyes severe and beard of formal cut,
Full of wise saws and modern instances;
And so he plays his part. The sixth age shifts
Into the lean and slippered pantaloon,
With spectacles on nose and pouch on side,
His youthful hose well saved, a world too wide
For his shrunk shank; and his big manly voice,
Turning again toward childish treble, pipes
And whistles in his sound. Last scene of all,
That ends this strange eventful history,
Is second childishness, and mere oblivion,
Sans teeth, sans eyes, sans taste, sans everything.

            Shakespeare

CONTENTS

	Prologue	9
	Section 1: Protection	
1.	The First Decade	15
2.	The Second Decade	33
3.	The Third Decade	53
	Section 2: Forgiveness	
4.	The Fourth Decade	77
5.	The Fifth Decade	95
	Section 3: Serving	
6.	The Sixth Decade	113
7.	The Seventh Decade	129
8.	The Eighth Decade	147
9.	The Ninth Decade	157
	Section 4: Served	
	Post Script	165

SECTION ONE

Protection

"But the Lord is faithful, and he will protect you from the evil one."
2 Thessalonians 3:3

CHAPTER ONE

The First Decade
1910-1920
Age 0-10

"He tends his flock like a shepherd: He gathers the lambs in his arms and carries them close to his heart; he gently leads those that have young."
Isaiah 40:11

January 5th, 1910 in central Indiana was much like one would imagine it to be for that time of year. Only in the Midwest can the weather be so different in the span of twenty-four hours. The day started out as one of those nasty, cold, wet, dark and dreary days. The temperature was hovering just at the freezing level making it nearly impossible to move about without suffering from either the cold or some sort of accident with whatever mode of transportation one chose to use. Everything in the world seemed depressed because the weather made everyone feel lost.

As the day progressed the weather improved consistently. The sun managed to make its way from behind the clouds and warmed the earth to a point where the ice and snow began melting away and the energy from the sun made everything in the world seem right again.

The day seemed to be God's table of contents for the life that would be started on that day. George W. Huff, "Joe", as his father and others came to call him, became a part of the world early on that morning in January. No one present at the birth could have predicted just how closely the course of Joe's life would mirror the weather of that day.

To say the early days of Joe's life were cold and depressing is really an understatement. His family was of German descent and his father was a blue-collar worker trying to scratch out a means of survival for his wife and children. Poverty was a way of life for Joe in the early years and even though many others were in the same predicament, most were not nearly as poor as the Huff family.

Guy, Joe's dad, was a small man who seemed much larger than his 5'6" frame stood. Maybe it was his barrel chest and thick hair, but the small stature man seemed to tower over those in the family when it came to his personality. To say he was a bit on the rough side would not be strong enough. Having come over from Germany and having to literally fight for the little he had, Guy had developed a demeanor which caused many much larger than he to back away from any confrontation. This included his wife of nearly ten years.

When Guy spoke, most listened, and if they didn't he could make his voice rise to a level that could not be ignored. Also as the level of the voice rose, so did the frequency of the vulgarities. Words that most would never think of using became "normal" for Guy if the intended listener did not take him seriously.

The day their first child came to be a part of the Huff family was an example of Guy's violent temper and his self-centered personality. When Georgia, his wife, informed him she thought it was time to deliver the new child, Guy became agitated. It was as if she was putting him out. Why couldn't she have more control over the situation? After all, didn't she realize how bad the weather was out there? Guy, like many other times past and future, would finally realize his error and apologize, but unfortunately only after the hurt had already been inflicted and unable to be reversed. January 5th was one of those occasions and possibly the beginning of the end of the marriage.

On this cold day in January, Georgia was hopeful that the new baby would wait until the weather improved. After all, the midwife had to travel there and with the freezing temperatures and the ice and snow; it could make her arrival very difficult.

The First Decade

The pregnancy had not been an easy one, anyway and if there was no one present to help deliver this child, Georgia had the uneasy feeling things would not go well.

It seemed this day of the baby's arrival was an icon of Georgia's life. There was much despair and not much hope. Georgia had thought that bringing a baby into the picture would make things better, but so far all she had seen from Guy was more emotional outbursts rather than fewer. The most recent being just today when she reluctantly told him the baby was coming and he lashed out at her for her poor timing. Her lack of control over when the baby came was much like the lack of control she felt over all her life during this time.

Whether or not she wanted this child to come, come he did and into a house seemingly divided. The physical setting that Joe came into was something out of a nightmare. The house was old, cold and heated only with a small coal-burning stove in the small living room adjacent to the kitchen. The only other room in the rented house was a small bedroom where Guy and Georgia slept.

The neighborhood was one of poverty, crime and desperation. Men and women tried to scratch out a life for them and their families, but there was not much happiness or hope. Guy and Georgia's life seemed to be even on the low side of this lower east side community in Indianapolis, Indiana. Challenges were around every corner in the neighborhood and in Guy and Georgia's life. The hope that bringing another life into the world would somehow make it better was not to be realized. All the birth of Joe did was to further increase what was an already complicated life of two desperate souls. Just as trouble seemed to be around every corner for Guy and Georgia, the same was to hold true for the life they brought into their relationship, community and world. As Joe's life mirrored this day of January 5th, his early years mirrored the troubled community into which he was placed by birth.

Joe's journey through life was underway albeit in the humble dwellings of Guy and Georgia. Each of the first three years were one much like the other with little food, moves from one dwelling to another because of no money to pay rent, and frustrations over the struggles of everyday existence. Both wanted more, but neither had a clue of how to make their lives different. These were the earliest memories of Joe, of his mother and father fighting, his father being angry and storming out of the paint-less, cold, miserable place they called home.

Just when Georgia and Guy both thought things couldn't get any worse, Georgia found out she was pregnant with her second child. Guy was not happy about this latest development to say the least. Just as on the day when Joe was born and he blamed Georgia for her poor timing, he blamed her again for this pregnancy as if he had no part in the process.

Guy had managed to secure what he thought would be a job which could finally get them to a point of being able to survive with some consistency. He would be working at the local dairy delivering milk and other dairy products around town. Georgia's announcement sent Guy into a fit of emotion and depression that with another mouth to feed, they would be lucky to maintain their present life, let alone improve their conditions in any significant way as he had hoped.

Joe, being only three, took the news of a new brother or sister much differently than did his parents. Being so young, he didn't yet realize how desperate the situation was and all he cared about was having a playmate he could count on to always be there. Each time in his yet short life he had a friend, his family moved and the friend was no longer there. At least with a new baby sister or brother, there could be a more permanent friend by his side who would always be with him filling the void left behind as a result of his family's transient lifestyle.

The months of pregnancy for Georgia were not easy. She seemed to be sick and on edge more and more. The months of waiting for the new member of the family were not filled with the joy most would feel, but more with sorrow of what was to come. Another mouth to feed and another responsibility heaped on Guy's head. It was as if during these months instead of growing closer together, the two seemed to grow farther apart.

Along with the trauma and sickness of the pregnancy came the everyday trials and tribulations of raising a young son. Joe was a very active and adventurous young boy. His innate desire to "push the envelope" when it came to his play, combined with the fact that few things provoked fear in him, many times led to interesting predicaments. On one of the "routine" days of existence for Georgia, a near tragedy was averted.

> *Back to my earliest recollection I know that evidently the good Lord was watching over me that as a very, very small boy my mother had done the washing and had the clothes line up in back and right at the door she always put a loop and there were about three steps going down and I went out. It was before I was even going to school, and I went out and I put my head through the loop and stepped off the steps. My mother was at the back fence talking to the neighbor lady and she happened to look up and she says, "My God look at that child!" I was black in the face. I was almost dead when they took me down. So I know my Lord was watching over me. Of course I didn't realize at this time that He had a purpose for my life.*

When it was time for the second child to come be a part of the family, it was much different than the day Joe was born. The day was sunny and bright, but the weather did not reflect the mood of the family. Georgia was apprehensive about the birth after all the trouble she had while carrying the child and Guy seemed to want to run as far as he could from the event. The memory of the Titanic tragedy was still fresh in everyone's mind and Guy's sense of hope seemed to sink as quickly as the Titanic.

The birthing room was not what one would think of today. Instead of clean, white, sterile conditions the room to welcome this new life was a small, simple bedroom in another run down rental property on the southeast side of Indianapolis, Indiana in 1913. The bed was an old feather bed and when Georgia finally knew it was close to delivery time and lie down in the bed, it was as if she was swallowed by the mattress.

Guy had gone to get the midwife to help with the delivery and the three year old, wide-eyed Joe knew something was happening, but he was not sure exactly what. He knew his mother was in pain because he could hear her screams getting louder and louder. His father had told him he must stay away from the bedroom where his mother had taken refuge.

There had been water boiling on the stove for quite some time. Joe's mother had planned to do the weekly wash that day, but the coming of the child had stopped her normal routine. Before Guy left to bring back the much needed help of the midwife, he had placed the tub of boiling water on the floor beside the stove and totally forgot he had left it unattended with an unsupervised three-year-old in the house.

For some reason Joe stayed away from the stove and the water, but the continuing screams of his mother, which got louder and louder even after the midwife arrived, both scared and intrigued Joe's three-year-old mind. He couldn't resist sneaking over to the door and peeking through the crack just at his height and looking into the scene of his mother screaming and the midwife attending to and coaching her through the natural childbirth. He became so involved in the scene he failed to hear his father come up behind him. In one motion, Guy lifted Joe off his feet and threw him into the old chair that sat beside the bedroom door.

After a severe tongue-lashing Joe retreated to his area of the old house and waited for what seemed like an eternity. Then the sounds of his mother's screams were replaced with a new sound. It was still screaming, but tiny screams of the newborn child. Edna, Joe's little sister, had come to be a part of the Huff family.

There is no worldly explanation for why the Huff family did

not lose a child the same day one came into the world. Putting a tub of boiling water on the floor in front of a three-year-old boy was like inviting him to an exciting aquatic adventure. Yet Joe miraculously stayed clear of the looming danger. Even at this young age, God was beginning to protect Joe from the harms of the world, and most importantly, protecting him from himself.

From the time Edna was born, Joe had a special affinity for his little sister. Despite the normal raucous playing of a three-year-old boy, he had a sense for when she needed something. He always seemed to just "appear" by Edna's side whenever she started crying and even though there wasn't much he could do for her he was there looking out for her best interests and making sure everything was all right. When Edna started taking solid foods, Joe loved to help his Mom feed her. Joe often fed Edna with one of the little silver spoons that had been given by their maternal grandmother in honor of each child's birth.

As Edna began to walk and communicate, Joe started including her in his playful activities more and more. There were never many toys around like some other kids might have, so the two were forced to be creative with the little they had. Their lack of material possessions drove them closer together and the two quickly became inseparable.

Another dynamic that impacted their relationship was the environment in which they lived. The trials of life were starting to take a toll on Guy and Georgia. Guy worked long hours and still couldn't get ahead of their depressed financial state. The relationship between them became more and more tenuous by the week. The result was a recurring theme of arguments and unrest around the house. Joe and Edna sometimes became the brunt of their parents' frustration. To avoid the usual dysfunction when Dad got home, Joe would take his little sister's hand and lead her to the back room of the house where they would quietly play until tempers subsided and it was safe to emerge again.

At the young, impressionable age of six, Joe was an unwilling participant in an event the details of which would stay emblazoned in his mind forever. Despite the best attempts to direct loved ones and others away from harm and pain, only the protection of God is sovereign. It was evident that God had chosen to spare Joe when his father left the boiling water on the floor in the rush of events the day Edna was born. Yet in the routine of everyday life, God chose to allow a tub of water to now play a very tragic role.

One of the great mysteries and struggles of life is coming to grips with human mortality, especially as it relates to children. What is even harder to accept is that God's control over mortality is perfectly just and omniscient. With all the depravity around Joe at this point in his early life, what he needed most was his little sister by his side. He needed someone to share his days with, someone who loved him and accepted him and appreciated his company. For reasons beyond human comprehension, God decided that it was time for Edna to come back to His eternal care. Maybe in His infinite wisdom, God chose to spare Edna what was sure to be a difficult childhood. For whatever reason, God took her back without a moments notice. There was no time to prepare, no time for a final hug or kiss or even a simple good-bye. What made the event even more devastating for Joe was it happened as he was doing what he always did; trying to care for his little sister.

...I was six years old. I can remember this vividly even though many years have passed. I was in the kitchen and my little sister (Edna) who was 3 years old was with me. My mother had put our wash water on the cook stove. Back then we used stoves that we cooked on that held coal. The tub that she had put on the stove was for our Sunday night baths. My father had gone to town and had just returned and my mother and dad had taken the tub off the stove and had placed it on the floor. I was at the kitchen table up on a chair on my knees and I was fixing bread and jelly. I had fixed a piece and I held it out to my little sister. Instead of coming towards me and receiving the bread and jelly, she backed away

from me smiling and she was just tall enough that the tub hit her right at the knees and she fell over into the scalding water and she was scalded to death. This is something that I shall always retain in my mind... the screams and the agony that we went through at this time.

The bookends of Edna's life in Joe's memory were her screams; the screams of her birth that were joyous and hopeful and the screams of her death that were filled with agony and sadness. Though he had no way of conceptualizing it at the time, all the while God was protecting Joe for another time and another task.

Joe's life many times was much like other boys of his age and his background. Joe lived in a racially mixed neighborhood. He lived with others of different color but all of the same, or basically the same, economic backgrounds. Joe's family, just as his neighbors, struggled for every small material gain to make their lives more bearable. It is interesting that the Oreo cookie was first manufactured around this time. While Joe and his friends could only afford to buy the new cookie once in a while as a special treat, the neighborhood reflected the make-up of the cookie itself. Joe's neighbors on both sides of him were African-American while he and his family were Caucasian.

In Joe's words he gives us insight into his neighborhood.

...And as we go along, I can remember that we have so much trouble now with racial differences but then I know that we had an African-American family that lived in back of us who had two boys and we played together continually. I would either go to their house or they would come to my house. Often times I would eat at their table or they would eat at my table and we played with different children, especially one girl that I can remember and she was African-American and they all used to kid me that she was my girl. Of course as a child then I didn't want girls and didn't even think anything about them and so I

always got kind of angry because I felt they were taking advantage of me, but this is one of the things that comes to my mind.

Joe relates another story of his mixed neighborhood. When walking home from school he called out to some of the African-American girls and used a name they didn't appreciate. He referred to them as a specific kind of candy and they began to chase him all the way to his front door. He did manage to outrun them, but not without dropping all his belongings on the way. He dashed to the house, ran to his room and dove under the bed. The girls didn't give up their chase and came to the front door and yelled for him to come out and face them. Georgia, protecting her son, sent the girls on their way. As happens with most children, the next day, Joe admitted his mistake and he and the girls mended their differences and were once again good friends.

Guy was not as understanding as Georgia. Joe's interaction with others in the community did not always sit well with his father. On more than one occasion, Joe found himself in the coal shed taking the brunt of his father's rage for an interaction with some other boy or girl in the neighborhood. Even in this time of punishment, God was protecting Joe, as Guy would somehow always stop short of hurting Joe severely. It was as if God would say enough is enough and takes Guy to another thought or action.

One such occasion happened when Joe was coming home from school and one of the neighborhood boys decided he was going to "take care of Joe." Guy was not satisfied with the way Joe handled himself and took action. Joe believed this event could have been one that started him on the road in the "wrong direction."

...Then coming home from school one day I shall never forget I was always told that I shouldn't cause trouble, but I don't know why this 'fella decided that he was going to take care of me so he

hauled off and punched me in the nose. Well, I just turned around and walked home and when I got home my parents looked at me and said, "What's the matter with you?" and I started cryin.' And they said, "What happened?" and I told them and my dad, as I said had a very, very violent temper, and he took me by the hand and he took me right back down there and the boy was standing in his back yard and he called to him and he said, "Come out here!" and the boy came out and my father looked at me and said, "You either whip him or I'll whip ya.' I'll whip you!" So there was no alternative because I knew how my dad whipped. And I piled into him and I just beat the tar out of him. But back then we had woodsheds on the back of our property where we kept coal and stuff and my dad, whenever he punished me, he always took me by the arm and took me to the coal shed and when I made that trip I knew what was coming because like I say he had a very violent temper. So during my boyhood even coming up at that time it seemed that I was heading in the wrong direction, the direction that I shouldn't have been going....

That fact that this episode had such a profound impact on Joe points to an important aspect of his character. Being forced to hurt someone else went directly against his nature. In his heart of hearts, Joe naturally had a caring spirit toward others. It is obvious all Joe was seeking was someone to just ask if he was okay and help tend to his wounds. Unfortunately, what happened was just the opposite. His pain from being wrongly hit was only compounded when he had to fight back against his will. Much like what happens as a result of a physical injury, this episode caused a numbing layer of scar tissue to form over this newly created wound in the young boy's heart.

The Ford Motor Company entered into Joe's life at different times in different ways. As America gained momentum in the modernization of manufacturing, Henry Ford made a contribution that helped the common man including Guy Huff. The invention of the assembly line in the manufacturing of automobiles back in 1913 allowed the average working man like Guy to own an automobile. As a result, society as a whole had become more mobile.

Guy had an older Model T Ford, which required cranking to be started. This was despite the fact that the electronic ignition had already been conceived and many cars around town no longer required cranking like the Huff family car. As with most other areas of Guy's life, this predicament led to much frustration. On one occasion as a young elementary aged boy, Joe remembered watching his father attempting to start their Model T. It was a cold day, and as he often did when it was cold, Guy took a teakettle of boiling water and poured it over the manifold to warm the engine. His efforts failed so he tried jacking up the car off the rear wheels, another method often employed with cars of this era. As usual, circumstance was toying with Guy's emotions and nothing was working. As if the car had ears and feelings, Guy began swearing uncontrollably at the hunk of metal. Finally as a last resort, he hauled off and kicked the ten-year-old car and gave it one last crank. It started, much to the surprise of Guy and his young son looking on. Years later, Joe considered the story humorous. But at the time what could have been an opportunity for father and son to share in a challenge of overcoming adversity instead turned into a sobering display of a man's frustration. Guy's bad temper and constant use of profanity forced Joe to address the issue with a level of maturity not normally required of a young boy.

> *...Then I can remember also that as a boy my father, I hate to talk about my father, but this is the truth. My father was a man that he couldn't draw two breaths without swearing one. This upset me I can remember as a child that this upset me very much because it sounded terrible to me and I didn't like it so I made a vow to myself, even as a small child, that if I grew up and got married and had a family that I would never use profanity in front of my wife or my family. Now this may sound funny as a small child*

The First Decade

but this was something that was impressed upon me that I shall never forget the vulgarness of the swearing and so forth and so on that was done in my presence that shouldn't have been done because it made a mark on my life that I can say was for the better and not for the worse.

It may not have been that Guy and Georgia didn't love their son, but rather they didn't know how to express it. They did not have the love of God in their hearts and therefore could not show the love they themselves had not experienced. Whatever the reasons, the lack of love toward Joe was also evident in the lack of love and the growing distance between Guy and Georgia. The relationship was becoming more and more strained on the way to a final termination. In the interim, however, Georgia and Guy had another futile attempt to strengthen the marriage one of the only ways they knew how, by trying to bring more lives into the world; all this happening with no relationship to God. This pattern continued on two more occasions.

In 1917, Joe's seventh year on the earth, slightly over a year since Edna's tragic death, Georgia delivered twin boys. The first was born dead and the second lived only about an hour. Joe was able to hold the one living brother for only a few minutes before the precious one went to join his brother and Edna to be with the Lord.

It was only a short time later that once again Georgia became pregnant. The futility of trying to bring another life into the world to mend the relationship was something neither could see. They were blind to the real void; that of not having Christ in their lives and as many do now, they tried to fill that void by human measures rather than Godly ones.

A positive about this particular child coming into the world was that she was born healthy and would end up living a productive life with a solid relationship with Jesus Christ. Charlotte Huff came to be a part of the household October 1, 1918. One would think that finally having the sibling Joe had longed for in the beginning of his life would now have brought him some peace and comfort. That did not seem to be the case however. For some reason, Charlotte coming into the already tough financial situation simply made life even tougher for the entire Huff family. In order to be away from home more as well as trying to supplement the meager income of the family as a whole, Joe began to go work with his grandfather in his barbershop. Being exposed to an adult environment on a regular basis at only nine years of age caused Joe to begin his slide to an early life filled with trouble and strife.

The barbershop hearkened back to the day of the spiraling red and white barber sign, salty conversation and full service. There were three identical chairs in the shop and three completely unique personalities in the men who stood behind them tending to the hygiene of their customers. Being on the corner of a near east-side street in downtown Indianapolis, the clientele ranged from the hourly worker scraping to get by to the well-known politicians and other social elite.

In the back of the shop, separated by a partial divider, were two large bathtubs where Joe spent much of his time working. His main job, apart from shining shoes, was to keep the bathtubs and the back room clean for the patrons. His work was centered in the bare essence of serving others. These patrons were the roughest of the lot. Mostly railroaders coming in from long trips, they would come through a rear entrance to the shop and use the facilities to bathe and make themselves presentable for whatever upcoming activities they would be undertaking in the big city. Joe would make his way around the shop hardly noticed, being so young and small of stature. Even though his frame gave away his youthful state, his mind and ears were hard at work picking up on the content of the adult conversations going on around him.

At this time, Joe also began to become acquainted with some of the physical maturities of life. At the ripe age of nine, without any of his own encouraging, Joe got his first shave in one of the barber chairs at his grandpa's shop. So with a cleanly shaven face what else was a young boy to do, but go out into the world and claim for himself a young dame to be his girlfriend—and that was exactly what Joe did. Being among the wage earning population, Joe headed down to the neighborhood drugstore one day with a shiny nickel in his pocket and proceeded to acquire a china doll for his fair maiden. These innocent qualities of affection and devotion for his first "girlfriend" revealed the true character that even then God was shaping in Joe's heart. Amidst the rough adult world around him, there was a gentle spot inside that God had created for a time to come. If only someone could have been there for Joe at this time to nurture these positive traits and develop them more completely, he may have been spared the emotional pain that future relationships would bring in the coming two decades of his life.

Guy, Georgia, Joe and Charlotte attended church on a regular basis in the early years of Charlotte's life. Even though they wanted a religious influence on their children, faith in God was not central to their family structure. If they could just get a better job, if they could just get a better house, if they could just have better things, life would be fine. They were empty and trying to fill themselves with worldly things rather than spiritual things. A mistake many make in today's world of plenty just as they did in a world of little.

Joe was exposed to many conversations while serving others at the barbershop. Some of the stories he heard would be considered ridiculous to those anchored in God's word. The fact that Joe and his family were so easily swayed by the undercurrents of everyday life makes the story of the "End of the World" Joe relates more tragic than funny. It seems there had been stories in the paper and talk on the street and in the barbershop that some so called "prophet" had predicted the end of the world on some specific day. Joe went to bed that particular evening with fear and trepidation that the end of the world would come before the next morning. Knowing that Joe was not yet ten years old at this time is helpful in understanding how he could believe this to be true.

At some time in the night Joe was awakened and his room was filled with a strange red glow. Of course Joe immediately knew this was what the people at the shop had been talking about and the end of the world was at hand. Joe immediately ran down to wake his father and mother. As Guy slowly leaned up on one elbow and saw his young son, wide eyed and terrified, he cursed at him and told him to go back to bed and leave them alone. Joe was persistent even in the fear of reprisal from his father and pleaded with him to "just look out the window!" When Guy and Georgia finally did they too saw the same strange red glow that Joe did. They now became as frightened as Joe because they had heard, but had dismissed, the same stories in the paper and on the streets.

If only they had the peace and promise of Christ in their lives, they could have been joyful even if it had in fact been the end of the world, but they were terrified because they did not have the promise of eternal life. As it turned out, the red glow was real, but rather than being the end of the world, it was the end of the neighbor lady's distillery. She liked to drink and since Prohibition was in, she had decided to make her own liquor and her 'still (her hen house) had gone up in flames. Knowing where Joe's life was going, one could draw a real comparison to Joe's life and the lady's hen house. Alcohol destroyed her hen house and it would nearly do the same to Joe in the years that lie ahead.

At the end of Joe's first decade on this earth he had already lived through more tragedy and strife than many do in a lifetime. He had lost loved ones, been verbally and physically abused and lived a life of poverty and pain. All this time, however, when one looks back the hand of God could be seen protecting and providing for Joe in circumstance after circumstance.

The year was 1919, Prohibition had just been enacted and Joe was seemingly trapped and unfulfilled in his present setting.

He decided to go and live full time with his grandfather and grandmother. His parents and Charlotte were moving once again and he wanted to stay and attend school in the part of the city where he was currently living and spend more time working at the barbershop. World War I was over, but the war with Satan had just begun in earnest. Joe didn't even know at this time, but the match for his soul was only at the beginning stages.

Joe and Edna

CHAPTER TWO

The Second Decade
1920-1930
Age 11-20

"For I know the plans I have for you," declares the Lord, "plans to prosper you and not to harm you, plans to give you hope and a future."
Jeremiah 29:11

The second decade of Joe's life was ushered in much like the first was left behind; with tragedy around every corner and God's protection more and more evident. It was also a time when history ushered in the "Roaring Twenties." The Charleston dance was bursting on to the scene as was more and more of the "modern" conveniences of life.

Life seemed to be changing at warp speed. The first radio broadcast would be heard as well as Lindbergh's trans-Atlantic flight. Penicillin would be discovered to heal many diseases, but it couldn't protect Joe from the evils of life's experience he was about to live through.

Whether the environment caused Joe to be caught up in the evil and revelry or Joe just contributed to the perception of the time by adding to the less than acceptable behaviors, the reality was that as the decade of the twenties progressed so did Joe's plunge into the seedy, worldly side of life. He made no excuses for his plunge other than his mistake of listening to Satan's voice rather than the voice of the Holy Spirit. In some sense, Joe was like the Bible character King David in that even though he strayed and committed many sins, God protected him through the years because God's plan was bigger than Joe's mistakes. Joe, over and over again makes the point there was nothing glamorous about this time. He would have no one believe they would or should have these kinds of experiences; it is just what he chose to live through before he finally realized what God's love and grace could do in his life. Just as God protected David in his times of trouble, He also protected Joe so the life he would lead after submitting to God's authority could have impact on literally hundreds of others.

Early in the first year of the second decade of Joe's life another of the many tragedies occurred. His father, who had earlier landed the job at Banquet Milk Company, was struck by a truck and severely injured. This was a time before the hospital and medical community was where it is today and also before the health insurance that we all take for granted. Guy was "patched up" the best he could be and sent home to have the severe injury to his hip heal. The problem was the healing did not go as expected. Even though Georgia tended to his wounds, Guy was totally an invalid in every sense of the word. He became rather than the family provider, the anchor that was dragging down an already sinking ship of a family. Georgia was a healthy woman who had great burdens financially and physically, and there was some question in Joe's and other family members' minds that Georgia may have begun to stray into the waiting arms of her soon to be second husband, Arthur, during this time.

Even though Georgia may have been straying away from the long troubled marriage to Guy she still never wavered from her attentiveness to her children. Charlotte and Joe were always under her watchful eye, or at least she thought so. Joe had long ago made his vow that he would never curse, as did his father. At this early age, however, he really didn't know all the words he was not supposed to use. On one occasion, Joe was playing with some new friends who had just moved into the neighborhood. One of the boys got angry and used the four-letter word. Joe, even though he had made and kept his vow, went home and when Georgia said something to anger him, he came back with the same new word he had just heard. To say that Georgia reacted was an understatement.

> ...*I did not know the meaning of it and had no idea what the meaning of it was so when I came into the house my mother said something to me and I made the same remark to her which I shall never forget because I was very soundly spanked and I was told never, never to say that word again. Of course like I said I had no idea what the word meant or what it was meant to be, but I heard the word so I used it as the other boy had used it. This taught me a lesson to never repeat the things that I heard unless I knew exactly what I was talking about.*

Joe using the four-letter word was only a hint of the worldly events to which he would soon be exposed. He didn't know what the word meant at this early age, but others around him most certainly did and would begin to influence his life in a very negative way.

Often times in one's life, sin has a way of multiplying itself. A soul out of alignment with God will become more and more corrupt if it is not kept in check. Satan wants man to be as devoted to him every bit as much as the Heavenly Father wants man to be in His will. At any point in life each will be on one side of the fence or the other. Joe's side of the fence in 1920 was the dark side. The side with high grown weeds and trash scattered about. The boards of the fence needed a new coat of paint and others needed to be replaced. At least that is how it appeared on the outside. In Joe's soul, the war waged on for the young man's allegiance to either good or evil.

For a young man roaring into the stage of adolescence, one of Satan's most powerful weapons is the opposite sex. And at this point in his life, Joe possessed nothing of the armor of God. He was virtually defenseless. Time after time, Joe was presented with the lure of physical temptations. Without proper guidance from adults in his life, he was offered no alternative but to experiment with the various ways of the world. As the owner of the wrong side of the fence began launching an offensive, he picked just the right way to start the vicious cycle of multiplying sin in Joe's life.

Many times and in many forms, the troubles of physical promiscuity came looking for Joe and he went looking for them. It all started with a young girl who knew more than her age should have allowed. Her family lived through a field behind Joe's house. As the adults were conversing with one another, the kids went off to play and Joe found himself being summoned to the hayloft by the oldest neighbor girl. She proceeded to introduce him to things of the flesh, thus beginning a cornerstone of sin in his life that would carry on for years to come.

Now that Satan had won a battle, he got the perfect opportunity to capitalize on it. Guy's condition was continuing to put a strain on his ability to provide for the family. In 1921, when Joe was eleven years old, his family was forced to move. Because of his relationship with his grandparents, working in the barbershop and attending school, Joe was allowed to stay and live with his grandparents. The worse thing that can happen to someone when struggling with sin is to have no accountability and that is just the situation where Joe found himself. He was about to have even more freedom in his life. Little did he know that he was now fully exposed to his enemy and the difficulties were only beginning.

Now that Joe was with his grandparents all the time his relationship with them grew stronger and stronger. They were much older, however, and their ability to control and discipline Joe was nearly non-existent and the little effort they put forth only lessened as Joe moved into his teenage years.

While still at the formative age, his body came under attack in more ways than just the sexual prowess of the young ladies of the community. Joe spent so much more time now in the barbershop; he began to notice the tantalizing art of chewing tobacco. The barbershop saw all the barbers, most all of the railroad workers who came into bathe and many of the everyday patrons with large bulging cheeks filled with the sweet nectar of chewing tobacco. At least that's what Joe thought. The barbershop had the smell of stale tobacco from the many bronze spittoons, and the remnants left from those who had missed the mark when aiming their projectiles of spent saliva into the waiting receptacles. One of Joe's jobs, after all, was to clean up these missed missiles off the floor and also to wash out the filled spittoons.

Joe had carefully watched where his grandfather's stash of fresh chewing tobacco was stored. Having spent all the time cleaning up the remnants of tobacco, one day Joe decided he should join in the "pleasure" of creating the mess himself. Joe describes the experience of his first encounter with tobacco in the following words

...Returning now to my grandfather's barbershop where I shined shoes...My grandfather always chewed tobacco and of course being a young kid, I chewed gum and so I always watched him. He had a big roll-top desk and he kept his chewing tobacco in this roll-top desk. Of course all the barbers chewed and had their spittoons all around. I had to sweep the floor and I had to clean the spittoons... This time I was walking past my grandfather's desk and nobody was looking, so I thought, so I reached in and grabbed a wad of tobacco and put it in the palm of my hand and I walked outside and there was a little place to stand on the outside. It was on East Washington Street in Indianapolis and I stepped back in this little cubby hole-like and I wadded the tobacco up and put it in my mouth and I started chewing. I no more than got it in there and chewed it up real good and my grandfather came to the door and said, "Joe, I need you in here." Well, here I had a wad of tobacco in my mouth so there was nothing else I could do, so I swallowed it. Of course you can understand what happened when you swallowed chewed tobacco. It doesn't sit very well on your stomach. That was one thing that I learned was not to chew tobacco.

The temptation of tobacco and other worldly vices continued to attack Joe from every corner. Because he was not in God's fold, Satan continued to pelt him with situation after situation. It may seem hard to comprehend how Joe could feel he was protected, but things could have been much worse than they ended up being.

The time Joe lived with his grandfather and grandmother did accelerate his experiences much like technology was accelerating. Even those who lived around the barbershop seemed to have been strategically placed by Satan to keep the carrot of the world's pleasures dangling in front of Joe leading him farther and farther into the depths of despair. One event involved the neighbors next door. The neighbors were two sisters, "old maids" in Joe's words, who shared the apartment adjoining the business. Joe's bedroom was directly across the alley from the bedroom of the two sisters. Each evening when Joe went to his bed, he was greeted with the vision of the sisters parading around their bedroom with no clothes on. Whether intentional or not, the image of two older women was always on the mind of the early adolescent Joe.

It was about this time that Joe began to search outside his family for some sort of structure. His mother and father had left him in the charge of his grandfather and grandmother and at their age, there was little structure. Just as with some young people today, Joe looked for structure and safety in a gang. He relates that when he tried to join his first gang he had to go through an initiation much like the ones that are still required today. Joe had to fight the leader of the gang. He didn't think it would have made a difference what the outcome was, just that he didn't back down from the fight. In reality, Joe "whipped" him, which caused him to be instantly on the inside of the gang.

Just as in today's society, there were rival gangs then as well. Joe was now entering his early high school years and becoming more and more involved in his gang activities. God showed His protection of Joe one specific night when a new rival gang came to his turf. He was still living with his grandmother and grandfather and they were not aware of what was going on in his life. Joe describes this brush with possible disaster.

> *I want to retract a little bit while my grandmother was still living and go back to the park that we were in. A bunch of us boys were up there one night and of course another gang moved in from another place and they were going to wipe us out.*
>
> *I never will forget these two great big guys; they started coming towards me. I was going to high school at this time and I took off running for home and they were right behind me. I made it to the house...and I had to go up several steps to get up to the house because it was on a small hill. I couldn't wait to open the screen door so I just went on through it. Of course I was chastised for that; for tearing up the screen door, but still it was better to tear the screen door up than me get torn up by these two big guys...*

Joe sums up some of his adventures with those he feared would hurt him during these trying times by quoting scripture:

> *"And fear not them which kill the body, but are not able to kill the soul: but rather fear him which is able to destroy both soul and body in hell." Matthew 10:28 KJV*

In contrast to some of the troubles he faced, Joe began doing some positive things that came naturally to him. God had gifted Joe with excellent athletic ability. He wasn't tall, standing at 5'7" but he was extremely quick on his feet and had tremendous strength for his size. He began playing football on the first team his high school ever had. He also started running track and quickly realized that athletics were one of the few positive reinforcements from which he could draw strength. Joe approached athletics with an unbridled passion. It was not uncommon for him during track season to run to the point of such exhaustion that someone from the school would have to bring him home.

This strong will and fortitude exemplified how Joe approached anything and everything he set out to accomplish.

Joe made his way around town in his early teen years. In fact, he referred to himself in the recordings of his life as a "Rounder." He was struggling with some of the same character traits as those being developed in any young person in the formidable years. With all the tragedy and unrest in his life, anger started to seep in to his being. His loneliness was increasing, having no one with whom to really share this stage of his life. His grandparents provided for him, but there was no one to help him work through all the emotions of trying to figure things out in the all-important transition of becoming an adult.

He recounted his struggles with anger in the following story. It also illustrates once again how his Heavenly Father was protecting Joe without realizing it. Despite all the things Satan was throwing in his path, God was seeing to it that Joe would not be permanently swallowed up by the world.

> *In high school I was quite a, what you would call, a "rounder." I was going to Tech then and I had quite a number of girlfriends and we went out and I also ran on the track team there. This one time I remember that I had just bought a new pair of track pants. They were white and very clean white and we were working out in the gym because it was cold out and we weren't allowed to go out in the cold. This one boy who was on the track team with me started making fun of me, and my white pants. I guess I had inherited a little bit of my dad's temper and I took just about all I could take and finally I grabbed him and I took him down on the floor. I was choking him and when the track coach pulled me off of him he was turning black in the face. For this I had to go to the Principal's office and I had to sit in the Principal's office every night until the office force went home. Then at the end of the month or so, I was taken into his office and I'll never forget; the man's name was Mylo Stewart. He was a very kind man who never raised his voice. He just looked at me and he said, "George,*

I want to tell you something. If you don't learn to control that temper, you're going to wind up in the penitentiary." Well, I learned to control it.

Most people can look back over their lives and identify others who have helped direct them in times of need. Such was the case in Joe's life with the principal of his school. With his reputation and history of causing trouble, Joe probably didn't deserve the extra time and grace Mr. Stewart took to try and help him. Perhaps he knew of Joe's rough home life and that he lacked a male role model at this time. It is also a reminder to the rest of us. Whether a teacher, a businessperson or fulfilling the role of parent or friend, one never knows when God may be placing someone in his or her path that is in need of eternal direction. He calls on all to be his voice, hands and feet in His service with the guidance of the Holy Spirit. There is no doubt Mr. Stewart's willingness to provide counsel to Joe at this critical time saved him additional pain in his already difficult life. This little act of kindness did something else for Joe. It woke him up to the realization that he needed a drastic course of action to address his anger problem. He needed some sort of safe haven in which he could try to build some positive momentum.

He found that haven in the sport of boxing. Boxing was the perfect way for Joe to redirect his negative thoughts, emotions and actions. Until he came to know the Lord, one of the themes in his life was always trying to place some barrier around himself that would serve as a source of protection and a frame of reference from which he could operate. The ropes of the boxing ring and the atmosphere of the gym served this purpose for the next eight years.

It seemed like, that after the Principal had called me down, I was going to do something about my temper which he had told me to do so I decided to take up boxing where I could get rid of my temper; I could take my temper out on something else. I went to train in the gymnasium and the man who ran the gymnasium was a very good middleweight, in fact he was right up at the top in the middleweight class. He even was going to fight the middleweight champ, who was Mickey Walker at that time. Something happened, I don't know what it was, something about the contract didn't go through or something, but anyway he was well enough up the ladder that he could do this. By working out in the gymnasium I could take my spite out on the bags or the punching bag or the heavy bag and by going through the exercises it took some of the worst out of me. And then later on I started climbing in the ring with some of the fellas there that hung around the gym and also the fighters who would come in from out of town who were going to fight in Indianapolis. I used to get in the ring with them. As a matter of fact, I climbed through the ring with just about everybody from any weight clear up to the heavyweight and I only weighed about 135 pounds. But I was very fast on my feet and very elusive and that's the reason they put me in, because these big guys couldn't hardly tag me. They couldn't get a hold of me.

It seems appropriate that Joe would mention Mickey Walker, someone who most likely was a role model for him. Joe could probably see himself in Walker's career. At 5'7" and 140 pounds, Walker was a spitting image of Joe in size and stature. Born in New Jersey in 1901 and fighting under the nickname "The Toy Bulldog", Walker is ranked by some as the third best Middleweight of all time and was in the prime of his career when Joe entered the sport. Walker was known as, pound for pound, one of the best fighters who ever entered the ring. Bearing another similarity to Joe, Walker was known for being strong and durable, willing to fight anyone and often getting into the ring with much heavier men.

While not having the spiritual tools he needed to defend himself, God was providing a way for Joe to fight against trials with his physical giftedness. This contradictory image of protection in the midst of aggression was something that defined Joe's character.

His younger sister, Charlotte, was now seven years old. The two siblings spent little time together because of Joe living with his grandparents, but on the weekends he often went home where Charlotte was the object of his affections and attention. It seemed Joe had already lived an entire lifetime worth of events since the death of his sister Edna just ten years prior, but he now repeated the same acts of protection for Charlotte that he showed during the few short years of Edna's life. His playfulness with her often consisted of getting down on his knees, putting the boxing gloves on her and having a little sparring session. The bond between the two continued to increase as the bonds in the rest of their family structure were coming apart at the seams.

As the love and connection between Joe and Charlotte deepened and strengthened, the disconnection between Guy and Georgia became more and more pronounced. The connection between Guy and Charlotte also seemed to be strengthening. Maybe it was because Guy, when the sickest, found he needed the love and care of others more than he ever realized he could. Guy's injury from being struck by the truck still required frequent attention. When Georgia tended to the wound she did so in a matter-of-fact manner as a task that needed to be completed. As Charlotte gazed at the exposed wound where light could be seen all the way through what had once been a healthy hip, Guy could see the love and concern on the small child's face.

It was at this time Guy's heart began to soften and his love began to shine through. His years of cursing, drinking and failure to love Georgia had already taken their toll on the marriage and relationship. Guy, even though partially healed, was still not able to support the family and Georgia had begun a possible relationship outside the bounds of marriage. Guy tried his best to salvage his family, but it was well past the time of being able to mend a relationship that had been so broken by time, poverty and tragedy.

At the final decision time when Georgia sent Guy out on his own he sat and cried and asked for another chance at reconciliation, but Georgia's mind was already made up. She was already deep into a relationship with Arthur Grant and planned to marry him as soon as the divorce was final.

Guy's heart continued to soften, but for whatever reason, the wound to his hip never healed. He still came to visit his daughter, Charlotte and faithfully picked her up each Friday so she could spend the weekends with him. Charlotte relates a memory of her father, Guy, standing in a black raincoat and black hat on a rainy, cold Friday evening. He was waiting patiently outside any shelter from the weather for his daughter's arrival from her day at school to the home that was once his. As soon as she greeted her mother, she picked up her few belongings and ran to be with the father she loved so much and it was evident the feeling was mutual.

Arthur's arrival into the family may have fulfilled the physical needs of both him and Georgia, but it did little to solidify a family in strife. Joe was not even an issue at this time and one could surmise that out of sight was out of mind. Little did Georgia and Arthur know that Joe's life was causing his grandmother and grandfather a great deal of concern.

A short two years after the final divorce, word came that Guy had finally succumbed to his injury of years before. He had times of relative health, but never to the point of being able to establish any sort of a new life for he and his children. It would have been his greatest wish to be able to undo much of the damage his life had caused, but it was not to be. He passed away on November 10, 1928. In one seemingly final measure to gain his son's forgiveness and acceptance, Guy made sure to leave his beloved car to his only son. Joe, not realizing the significance of this gift, accepted it, but did not appreciate the olive branch he had been passed.

Of course this loss affected all Joe's family, but none so much as the young sister he had grown to love so very much. It was all Joe could do to see what his sister was going through and what she had to live with. He continued to find his safety and security in things outside the Lord and in the bowels of Satan's lair. His relationship became more and more strained with his grandfather and grandmother. His late hours, lack of respect for his elders and his selfish behaviors did nothing to deepen a heart connection with his grandparents.

In the seemingly never ending tragic events of Joe's life a few, short months after losing his father, he came home following one of the nights out with his gang to find his grandfather weeping. His grandmother had passed and he hadn't even been aware of any illness from which she was suffering. This event seemed to be the gasoline poured on the fire of Joe's self-destructive path. Without the stable influence of his grandmother, he had no one to answer to and no one seemed to care. His grandfather came across as being very strict and punished Joe when he caught him doing something, but he never spent the same time loving as he did punishing. This just seemed to cause Joe to try more and more things. His mother was busy with her new life and husband, and his grandfather was just trying to survive without his helpmate of so many years. His young sister cared, but had no way to help him through this trying time of decisions for his life. Having a working grandfather as the one and only source of accountability for an eighteen-year-old young, rebellious boy was a blueprint for disaster for all concerned.

Joe's relationship with his grandfather was deteriorating quickly. Joe was still chasing girls, running with the wrong crowd and generally driving his grandfather crazy.

Even though his grandfather didn't know it, Joe was still having ample opportunities to explore the seedy side of life when it came to the opposite sex. One such occasion happened with the owner of the confectionary store next to the barbershop. The wife of the owner constantly tried to get Joe to engage in activity with her by exposing herself to him when her husband wasn't around. God's protection continued here, because

Joe never acted on the woman's advances. The lady was older and not the least bit attractive to Joe.

On one occasion, however, the owner and his wife were away and they had a baby sitter come to run the store and care for their young children. She called Joe over with the "ploy" of needing some help getting supplies off an upper shelf. She used the ploy as a way of exposing herself to Joe. With her seductive act, she had him basically convinced to follow through on her advances. Looking back on this event, Joe specifically mentioned this as a time when he knew beyond any doubt that God was protecting him. Just as the main event of this ritual was about to take place, his grandfather yelled for him to come back to work. This stopped the near encounter. Joe soon found out through his patrons at the barbershop that the young girl was infected with venereal disease and had infected many young men in the community. God had intervened in Joe's life to save him from what could have been a life-altering event.

It was also about this time that Joe discovered his next, and probably most destructive, vice to which Satan wanted to expose him. His first of many encounters with alcohol came at about this time of his life. Even though this was a point of time in history where alcohol was supposed to be prohibited, it was the time Joe first experimented. It was an experience, which put him on the fast track to, or near, becoming an alcoholic.

> *...My grandfather always made home brew and wine and such. He was very proud of his brews. Back then tonics and things came in gallon bottles and he used to wash them out and put his wine in them. This one time he had brewed up a big mess of wheat wine and it was an awful pretty color. He and I were living together because my grandmother had passed away. At this time we lived upstairs over the barbershop. He would at night, he would always take a drink out of his bottle and put it back in the refrigerator, well icebox, they didn't have refrigerators back then. Of course, being a kid, I watched him do that and I thought, "Well*

if he can drink that I guess I can too because I drink pop." So I poured out a water glass and I proceeded to drink it. You can understand what happened, I got very drunk and I got very sick. But of course this didn't teach me very much because you'll find out later on some things that happened that I didn't take heed to what I'd learned there.

For a person gifted with the ability to run fast and hard, Joe was living a bad dream of someone struggling with all his might yet merely running in place, unable to go anywhere in the game of life. He was searching all around for something or someone to break the bondage of his personal nightmare. He wanted to run free. He wanted peace, love and joy in his life, but no earthly means could provide it.

Several factors contributed to the next transition in Joe's life ensuring that he would continue running in place for some time to come. His introduction to the enticements of alcohol and the deaths of his father and grandmother prompted a change. His grandfather was growing ill with cancer of the mouth as a result of his many years of tobacco use. He was also grieving from the loss of his wife. At the same time, Joe's drinking and related behavior problems were on the rise. All this proved too much for his grandfather to bear. At the age of eighteen with his world crumbling around him, Joe was forced to move back with his mother and stepfather. This now meant living in a different part of town, a place where he had spent the earlier years of his life.

With only one-year left of high school, Joe had little time to find his place among his peers. He was able to reacquaint with some of his old friends and soon developed notoriety. This kind of fame, however, was not the kind that gets one into the National Honor Society, or causes an Ivy League school to come calling at the door offering a scholarship. Joe didn't have the sort of reputation that would get him elected Prom King. There was no clear course of direction for his next four years. No one had been saving money for his college. There was no frame of reference for him to realize that there was a world of opportunity out there for someone with his combination of loyalty, dedication and compassion for others. Instead, Joe found himself associating with a group of friends who encouraged him to build his reputation around things that went against the grain. Things that challenged any hint of authority structure that dared come his way. Joe continued to drink and have physical relationships with young women. His life was full and rich with experiences that the world might portray as glamorous. Today some might say he was living life "on the edge" and "taking control of his own destiny." In his own words, Joe describes this tenuous yet colorful period…

> *I think it was during this time that my grandfather had come to the place where he didn't want me around anymore because I was in too much mischief, so he decided to send me home to my folks. My stepfather was there then so I transferred from one high school to another… I enrolled in Warren Central. It was here then that I met my old friends that I had known when I had lived out in that district before… There were two of them especially and there wasn't anything that the three of us wouldn't do. So my first day in school I walked down the aisle and I had my mustache and the girls they were all oohing and aahing and so forth and so on…*
>
> *… So I was attaining another reputation in another school. Before I proceed I will tell you one time there was a girl who lived down the road from me and I asked her for a date. She said, "You know I shouldn't go out with you with the reputation you have." And I said, "Well that's alright with me," she says, "But I'll go." So you see even though you have a reputation there are others who want to take advantage of it…*
>
> *… I was young and full of vim, vigor and vitality and I was going fast down the wrong road and then started a problem that I later developed and that is the fellas and I we started drinking. We drank wine and we would carry pocket flasks to school. They called us The Three Bottle Babies…*

The Second Decade

With the same determination he used in athletics, Joe persevered and earned his high school diploma at the end of the second decade of his life. Survival, not education, was clearly the top priority for Joe at this time. However, God often has plans that are revealed in His timing. God had a plan for education to play a significant role in Joe's journey on this earth many years later.

Joe's life had gone through another decade of trials, tribulations and loss and absence of loved ones. All through his second decade and probably even more evident than in the first, God continued to protect and prepare Joe for what was to come. He still had a long journey to complete, but he was closer to finding the hope and love of Jesus Christ each day he survived in the years of his teens. The crash of the stock market happened on a black, bleak day in 1929, the end of the second decade of Joe's life. As the market tumbled, Joe's life seemed to be in a pile of ruins much like the now worthless stock so many had gained and horded. Joe's life was much like the market. He thought he was gaining through the events of his world, but in fact his life was crashing as well. Wall Street would come back stronger than ever and so would Joe, but it would just take him a bit more time. He would have to spend time away from home, have a failed relationship and continue to wrestle with the evils of alcohol in his walk toward the light of God's service.

SECTION TWO

FORGIVENESS

"…to open their eyes and turn them from darkness to light, and from the power of Satan to God, so that they may receive forgiveness of sins and a place among those who are sanctified by faith in me."
Acts 26:18

CHAPTER THREE

The Third Decade
1930-1940
Age 20-29

"But let all who take refuge in you be glad; let them ever sing for joy. Spread your protection over them, that those who love your name may rejoice in you."
Psalm 5:11

At the depth of the depression in the United States, Joe was also sinking deeper and deeper into his depressed state of life. In his own words he described his life at this time as event after event happened and trouble just seemed to find him wherever he was. Already through this time of being lost in the wilderness of the world, God seemed to be beginning the healing process in a small way. Joe recounts that during the Depression while living in the blended family, all attended church each Sunday morning. The interesting thing is Joe didn't attend with the rest of his family. He attended a different church for reasons only known to Joe. Perhaps it was that he didn't feel a real part of the blended family and even though he knew he needed to be in church, he didn't want to be there with them.

Whatever the reasons, this church attendance and the friendships with some of the young men who attended there launched another interesting part of Joe's story. Joe and these young men were not only a rowdy bunch, but they also had been given the gift from God to be able to sing. How this was discovered is a mystery, but the people of the community where Joe was living began to know and enjoy the singing of these young men. At a time when so many had so little to bring them joy, the sound of these young men walking back to their homes after a night of mischief was a welcome break from the hopelessness that many of the people living in the community experienced on a daily basis. This gift of a great singing voice would come back over and over again in Joe's life of service. When he shares in his own words from this time of his life, one can hear the joy he gets from describing how he used to entertain others with this gift.

> *...We didn't go out to look for trouble, but we never ran from trouble. We would get together and we would sing. All of us had good voices. We would walk to a park at night, which was several miles away just to get a drink of what we called "egg water." It was very bad smelling water, but we would drink it. We would sing all the way there and all the way back and people used to sit on their front porches waiting for us to go by to hear us singing because we did all have good voices and we had a good time, but here was the beginning of my alcoholic deal because we also drank very heavily which we shouldn't have, but we did.*

Arthur had lost his job, as many others had at this time in history, and the family had lost their home because there was no money to pay the bills. The emerging family moved to Indianapolis proper to a seedier side of town Joe refers to as "Little Chicago." Joe continued his relationship with old friends back in the other community and they continued to sink deeper and deeper into the world of illegal alcohol and their gang activities. Joe still had the car his father, Guy, had left him and when he could scrape enough money together for gas, or he had the time for the long walk to the other side of town, he would be there with his drinking buddies, the "bottle babies."

Even as God was protecting Joe, he was also protecting that precious little sister God had given him, Charlotte. On one specific day, Charlotte had in her mind that she was going to drive the car. After all, when her father, Guy was alive he used to sit her on his lap and she would merrily drive down the road. In her eleven-year-old mind she thought if she could drive on Dad's lap, she should be able to drive by herself. She hadn't thought through the dangerous ramifications of her actions. Joe had come in after one of his long nights out with his drinking buddies and left the keys in the car. Charlotte had watched carefully many times to see how the car was started and put into motion. The next morning she managed to sneak out and start the car. She had just begun to move down the gravel drive in front of the house, when she realized she was in big trouble. She had no idea how to stop the now moving projectile of steel.

God was protecting Charlotte on that day instead of Joe. This time, He used Joe as the protector. Showing the athletic body and fleetness of foot that God had blessed him with, Joe bolted from the house, ran beside the car and jumped onto the running board. He reached through the window and turned off the ignition bringing the car to an abrupt halt. This was not the first time, but a growing number of times Joe became the protector rather than the protected. During the forgiveness and service sections of his life to come, there would be more and more of these opportunities.

Joe's night out on the town and his subsequent absent-mindedness with leaving the keys in the car nearly led to another tragedy for him and his family. What started as an innocent experimentation with his grandfather's homemade wine not so many years earlier had evolved into the dark, bondage of adult sin. Joe's inability to control his drinking and his penchant for getting into street fights had once again brought him to the point of full exposure to the attacks of his hidden, true enemy—Satan. The safe haven of athletics that surrounded Joe during high school was no longer there. His spare time was dominated only by activities destructive to the mind, body and spirit.

The enemy was closing in on him and Joe could feel the presence of evil, he just wasn't aware of the source, or most importantly, how to fight it. Putting on his boxing gloves no longer gave him the same peace it did just a few short years ago.

The job market was bleak, if not non-existent, and the world was closing in around him. One more brush with disaster was all that Joe needed to decide it was time for another drastic change. Maybe another set of boundaries would change things and help free him from his life-dominating sin.

Things seemed to go from bad to worse because we just kept drinking more and more and more, which we shouldn't have done. Then my folks moved into another end of town, which was an enemy to the end of town that we lived in, and to get there I had to cross a bridge. Going home the first night there was a group of fellas on the other side of the bridge and they were all drunk. I walked across and one fella walked out and he called me a bad name which I let nobody call me and I hit him and I knocked him down. I just kept on walking and nobody said a word, they took it as it was. I thought to myself afterwards, they really could have killed me and thrown me out in the river and nobody would have ever found me probably. But, like I say, there was that protecting hand again. Then I decided that I wasn't doing any good there so this is when I joined the Navy.

World War I had ended twelve years earlier in 1919. The military was not currently engaged in conflict, which made Joe's decision to enter the Navy an easier one. By his reasoning, it would allow him the opportunity to have structure again. The boundaries he was always searching for. At the same time, the people who encouraged him into harm's way could be left behind. He could distance himself hundreds of miles away from the places that conjured up nothing but bad memories in his mind on a daily basis. So, armed with nothing but hope of better things to come, Joe headed off for times and places unknown. He would see parts of the world he never thought possible and meet people of all walks of life. What he didn't realize yet, is that geography is no limiting factor for trouble and evil.

During this first stint in the Navy, the Depression was still

The Third Decade

going on and Prohibition was still in place. Some were beginning to see the futility of the law, but others still hung on to the thought that people could be legislated out of drinking. As history shows, the one thing Prohibition did was to help organized crime get its foothold into society and men like Al Capone and John Dillinger became folk heroes for their criminal activities.

Joe actually had opportunities with the lifestyle he was living to come into contact in some minor ways with both men. While in the Navy he was stationed in Chicago and was still drinking as heavily or even more than before he left Indianapolis. In Joe's own words he relates how his thought of the Navy helping in his battle against evil did nothing but perhaps make it worse. Joe relates one such time when he had a brush with the seedy underworld of Al Capone.

Now the Navy was another new experience for me. I met people of all races and all kinds and all descriptions. We met women from everywhere that you could think of and all different kinds. Of course my drinking never got any better because one of the Petty officers knew where they kept the grain alcohol which was about the strongest thing you can get it at–100%. He would steal it and bring it up and we would put it in our coffee when we drank our coffee. ... It seems like here again things just went along this certain pathway because it was back in the time of Al Capone and we were in Chicago and were down on what they called the Fisherman's Wharf. A car had been parked over there with some fellas and girls in it. The girls came out and were talking to us and putting their arms around our necks and hugging us and so forth and so on. These fellas kept yelling at them to come and get in the car. Of course we couldn't understand what they were speaking about because they were speaking Italian and we didn't understand it, but they told us what they wanted so finally they got out of the car and they came over and they told us to leave the girls alone. We told them we weren't bothering their girls. This one fella told me he said, "You'll either leave them alone or else" and he pulled out a knife. That knife looked to me like a sword, I had never seen anything like it. There was a young fellow standing close by and he walked over and he started speaking to them. They talked back and forth in Italian for a while and finally they took the girls and went and got in the car and they said, "We'll be back" and I said, "We'll be waitin' for ya." So after they left this young fella turned around and he said, "If I were you boys I would go on. If you don't when they come back it will be bad." I said, "Well we're not afraid of them." He said, "No it would be alright if they fight the way you do, but they don't fight that way." So he took us down to one of Al Capone's joints and we got liquored up down there again. But it seemed like this was another time here that he could have cut me to pieces, to ribbons, but yet there was the Lord's hand.

The Italian mob may have deterred him a little, but it didn't keep Joe from using his fighting skills just a short time later in defense of one of his Navy buddies who had too much to drink. Today's social rules dictate having designated drivers and not drinking if under aged. The idea is to keep friends from harm's way by driving them home, hailing them a cab, basically just looking out for them. It all seems logical and progressive. Well, Joe's idea of helping out a buddy was quite different from merely having him "hand over the keys." It didn't have quite the preppy, modern feel to it that today's TV commercials try to convey. On this particular night of revelry in a Chicago Speak-Easy, Joe once again did what came naturally to him and took matters into his own hands—literally.

His buddy was getting real mouthy and the other patrons were quickly growing tired of it. Joe knew that they were on borrowed time and things were only going to escalate into trouble if he didn't step in and do something. There was added complexity to their situation because just merely being in this underground establishment in the dark recesses of some street in Chicago was blatantly illegal. Joe was feisty and never turned away from a fight, but he was also smart enough to know that a dishonorable discharge from the Navy wouldn't help his quest of turning his life around.

So what was a man to do? Well as usual, Joe's course of action was as surprising as it was hilarious. He dragged his buddy outside into the alley and proceeded to punch him in the face with enough force to win him the title belt in the middleweight division. With one blow, he had knocked his "friend" out cold. This course of action definitely kept them from getting into a bigger fight. His friend was "resting" in his new-found state of unconsciousness, but now Joe had a bigger problem that he hadn't thought of before the mighty blow. How was he going to get his buddy out of there and back to the ship? Yet again, Joe's creativity took over. Not wanting to spoil the rest of the night for himself, Joe just decided to leave his buddy right there where he lay and come back later to pick him up after having some time to regain his consciousness. So off Joe went to finish his night of fun with no concern for how his buddy would explain his busted face to the rest of the gang on deck the next morning.

After being stationed in the Great Lakes region for some time, Joe's ship received orders to set out and they began traveling to foreign ports of call. One of the benefits of serving in the military is the opportunity to visit other cultures and see sights that most people in their twenties don't get the chance to experience. As Joe reflected, he realized that the grips of sin in his life prevented him from seeing the richness of his surroundings at that time. Interestingly, some forty years later, God would allow Joe to right his mistakes and traveling would become a passion for him and an area of fulfillment. It was also here when he came to the full realization that the boundaries of the Navy were no help at all. He had managed to let another four years of his life go by and still there was no sense of direction and no purpose. Joe's words also indicate an increasing awareness and admission that he was battling something bigger than himself.

... and then we started traveling and we would hit different ports and instead of going around and looking at the scenery like we should, we would head for the nearest bar. So it just seemed to be one thing after another and, like I say, many times we were in scraps and we would get into a fight with sailors of other nations and so forth and so on. It just seemed like life was just one great big battle. We were in the middle of the battle and there wasn't even a war going on.

Joe's attempt at going to the Navy to gain boundaries and change his life had not worked at all. He was still searching for answers to life's problems, but was searching in man's arena instead of God's. Problems also continued to follow him all the way to Chicago and beyond. Even being away from Indianapolis, his past and tragedies continued to chase him. While away from home serving his country, he received the news that his grandfather, who had helped raise him and gave him his first job in the barbershop, had died. The cancer of the mouth had run its course and finally took the life of the Indianapolis barber. The constant chewing of tobacco which seemed such a natural thing in the early years of Joe's life now came back to take another one of his family members away from him.

All the things Joe had done in the past as far as boxing, singing, drinking and fighting all continued in those years in the Navy. Once he got the message his grandfather died all he could think about was getting out of the Navy and getting back home. It seems as time goes by it is easier to forget some of the real hurt and pain that has occurred in one's life, and that is the way it was with Joe. In his mind he had glamorized the times back home and looked at them through a lens of what he wanted it to be rather than what it really was. The lens he was looking through, however, had been tainted by Satan's lies.

When the time came that he could choose to re-enlist or go back to the streets of Indianapolis, Joe chose to go back. He tells us in his own words how quickly the transition back to the real versus his glamorized way of life took place.

The Third Decade

After my four-year enlistment was up, I came back home. I went back down to where I had lived before because that was where my folks were still living. I got back in with the old group and things started getting back in to the old shape again; drinking and carousing around.

Directed by his stepfather, Joe's parents had switched churches and were now attending an Episcopal church in town. In keeping with his usual individuality on the issue of religion, Joe chose to attend a different one, a Presbyterian church. He and the men he ran around with all attended, but they were a confused lot. Their Monday through Saturdays were filled with the usual shenanigans yet they became very involved with the church on Sundays.

The church provided Joe with the opportunity to use the singing voice he had discovered with his gang of friends prior to going to the Navy. Singing provided the only joy in his life during these years and in years to come it would provide for him in other ways as well. One of the most compelling attributes of God is His ability to use anyone at anytime to advance His message. God was using the vocal talents of Joe and his worldly band of merry men to lead worship in His house on Sunday.

This brief time was also pivotal for Joe in another way. The male mentor that Joe had been lacking in his life for twenty-four years had now been placed in his path. The minister of the Presbyterian Church took it upon himself to reach out to Joe and his friends.

We used to sing in church. We sang as a group, we sang as quartets and I sang with another fella in a duet. We really enjoyed being in church. We really enjoyed being with the minister. We all thought an awful, awful lot of him. Of course as usual, there were always things that we did that we shouldn't have done and the following Sunday morning, he would get up and he would hear about these things and he would preach on them trying to help us to understand that we were going down that wrong road and we should get back on that road that we belonged on. We appreciated the man; we really loved him as a man and as a minister…

The contrast between Joe's life on Sunday and the life he led the rest of the time was not a subtle one at all. For a quarter century now, Joe had been flirting with disaster over and over again, and God had been protecting him. Yet, as Joe recounted years later, trouble just kept finding him. It's hard to imagine the day after this next story that Joe tells, he could possibly have sung in his church with his minister/mentor by his side, but that could very well have been what happened.

Then again one evening I was going down, it was cold weather and I had my overcoat on. This man walked up to me and he said, "I've got a notion to shoot all the buttons off your coat." Well, you can imagine how I felt, so there was only one thing I could do. I said, "Well, let's go down and get a drink." So we went down to the tavern and went in, he was all for that. So I called the bartender back and I told him, "Be careful that guy's got a gun, he just threatened to shoot the buttons off my coat." He said, "I'll take care of it." So he went back up and asked the fella what he wanted and he started in, he said, "I'm going to take my gun and shoot all the bottles off the back bar." Well the bartender reached under the bar and grabbed the stick they used for packing down ice and hit him with it and knocked him clear across the room. The guy got up and went out and called the police (Joe chuckles). They arrested him for being drunk and carrying concealed weapons. Things like this they happened and it seemed that, like I say, that protecting hand was always there. And it just seemed like the Lord was with me although I didn't realize it at the time, and I didn't realize that he was taking this kind of care of me because he had a purpose for me.

So why was Joe still having these problems if he was so

faithfully attending church? The answer possibly lies in something that every individual who is confronted with a relationship to a holy God has to address. What does it mean to be a Christian? To someone who only saw Joe on Sunday he would have appeared like most any other person in the congregation, maybe even an example for others. The formula of the casual believer sure wasn't working for Joe, however, and the Bible tells us it won't work for anyone. God had one purpose in mind when he sent his Son on this earth to die for man's sins. He desires a personal one-on-one relationship with everyone.

Joe's minister was doing his part to bring this message to a man who had endured so much in his life, yet showed so much promise to be a positive influence for others. But for some reason, Joe had not internalized this. More specifically, the minister revealed something else to Joe that lit a spark deep within him. He demonstrated to Joe in striking ways what it meant to serve others. This characteristic of service was something that God had in mind for Joe from the start and was about to begin cultivating in his life in very real and personal ways.

> *Also it was the time that I met the man that made a good impression upon my life and that was the minister. It was a Presbyterian church. In the meantime, my folks had quit the Lutheran and went into the Episcopal Church, but I went to this Presbyterian Church. This preacher was a very kind man and he believed in doing things for others. There were very, very many poor families and he would go out and get furniture and things and we would deliver it for him. I went into homes where the only thing they had in the house was an old, dirty rug and a box sitting there for a table and little kids crawling around on the floor dirty with nothing to eat and it was really heart breaking. But I went in all kinds of environments that a lot of people didn't have to go through. It just seemed like God had planned for my life to let me see all sides of it. Of course, this is not the end of the story because there's quite a bit more but it seemed, like I said, that these environments were there.*

Although times were supposed to be better for the United States in general, people were still hurting financially and the recovery was happening quicker for those who had suffered the least rather than those who had suffered most. Those who managed to hold on to some sort of a "normal" life through those years of Depression bounced back quickly many times at the expense of those most affected. Several tried to grab at any means they could to crawl out of poverty and into the lifestyle they could see others had around them. Farmers who lost everything in the Depression and through the ravages of drought picked up their entire families and went searching for a better way of life much like Joe went searching in the Navy and through the artificial means of alcohol.

Even in Indianapolis, the blended family of the Grants and the Huffs was not immune from people trying to take advantage of those who were less fortunate. Many times desperate people succumb to desperate means to escape the plight life has dealt them. Arthur had still never landed that job which could raise the growing family from the ranks of the impoverished. Georgia, tired of living the life she had been forced to live, was vulnerable to any smooth talking con man who would choose to swoop down and devour the unsuspecting prey.

It is said if something is too good to be true then it probably is. This was the case when an eloquent, older man came to see Georgia and Arthur with a way out of their station in life. Georgia, having been so afraid she couldn't care for her young children, had set a plan in motion to have them placed in an orphanage-type home if she and Arthur totally bottomed out. This handsome, seemingly well-to-do man who showed up at their door might just be the ticket to their transportation out of the abyss of poverty and need. It seems he had seen Charlotte, then fifteen, and set his plan in motion. She was a brown-haired, blue-eyed girl who looked much older than the young adolescent she was. She was thin and very pleasing to the eye. The older, self-proclaimed wealthy man was taken with Charlotte and was willing to pay to have her be his bride. He spun a good tale of how he would care for her, send her to Europe for "proper" schooling and in exchange for the family giving up Charlotte, he would pay them very well for her to be his.

The deal had basically been completed when Charlotte was finally brought into the process. Georgia and Arthur had already agreed in principle and in payment with the wealthy aristocrat, but had failed to take in account the young Charlotte's thoughts and feelings. One could look at this instance and quickly judge Georgia and Arthur's motives, but most have not lived through what they had been suffering. They must have rationalized in their minds that Charlotte would be much better off since she would be escaping the traps of poverty. If she could help take them with her on the journey to the middle and/or upper class society, it would be a win-win for all.

Besides Charlotte's feelings and thoughts, the family had also not considered Joe's input into the scenario. Once Charlotte found out the plan, to say she was less than willing was a gross understatement. She let her mother and stepfather know, in no uncertain terms, she would have no part of being in an arranged marriage with a man more than thirty-five years her senior. The contract would still have probably been finalized had it not been for the entry of Joe into the picture. Charlotte went to the one person she could trust to save her from this fate. She went to her beloved Joe to rescue her from the situation for which she had no control.

Joe, in his direct, forceful manner went to his mother and stepfather and let them know in no uncertain terms they would not be sending his sister overseas with a fifty-year-old man. Whatever the reason; Joe's forceful presentation, God's intervention or a combination of both, Georgia backed down from her strong stance she had taken before and revoked the agreement. She was not happy she would be remaining poor, but at least she could keep a semblance of peace in the family by leaving Charlotte at home.

A few short weeks later the decision seemed much more of a God thing than a man thing. A newspaper article appeared with a picture of a man the family recognized staring blankly into the camera. It was the fifty-year-old "aristocrat" being led away in handcuffs by the police. The account in the news article revealed this man who had come to lift the Grants out of poverty by "helping" Charlotte to a better life was in fact a white slave trader. He had sold many young, poor girls just like Charlotte into the bonds of slavery overseas and had finally been caught.

Even though Joe had spent more time away from Charlotte and Georgia it was evident his love and devotion for them never wavered and in fact seemed to continue to grow. Later in life Joe continued to serve and care for Georgia up until the time of her death. To emphasize this, an event recounted by Charlotte herself occurred about this same time of the "slavery" incident. For some reason Arthur had decided to take out his frustrations of life on Georgia in a physical manner. He had her bent over the sink and was about to strike her when in walked her wayward son, Joe. In his calm, calculating voice and manner, Charlotte describes Joe grabbing Arthur and pulling him back away from the terrified Georgia. There is no way of knowing how many times this may have taken place in the past, but this was the last time it took place. Joe, in no uncertain terms, laid down the gauntlet to Arthur and made a sobering promise if he ever heard or saw Arthur touching his mother in anger, it would be the last thing he would ever do. Knowing Joe's heart it would be hard to imagine him killing anyone, but surely Arthur knew he would pay the price if he did not heed Joe's words.

After several attempts to secure full-time work to no avail, Joe was able to get a part-time job singing live on the air at a local radio station. Commercial radio broadcasts were still very new. It was 1935, three years before the famous airing of the Orson Welles radio broadcast War of the Worlds. Welles inadvertently created a nation-wide panic when he described aliens invading from outer space causing people to mistakenly take his entertainment show for an actual news broadcast describing the country under attack. Joe's impact, though not as dramatic as Welles', still influenced the few who heard his singing.

As usual, the job didn't come easily for Joe. With Guy's car now just a memory and without the means to own another or even to take the bus on a regular basis, he walked nearly two miles to work everyday and had to be at the radio station by 5:00 in the morning. In yet another indication of things to come, God used Joe to sing spiritual hymns during the religious portion of the station's daily programming. When he could scrape up enough extra money, he would take the bus to ease the burden of getting to work. After some time, the bus driver surmised that Joe was only riding when he had the money. The driver also came to realize where Joe was going and because he was singing religious songs, the driver found it in his heart to start allowing Joe to ride the bus for free. The driver was evidently one of those few who had been impacted by Joe's voice on the radio. The artistic ability that Joe had begun refining as a young man with his friends singing on the streets as they wandered about town was now putting bread on his table.

He also used this opportunity to branch out and further his singing career by joining a band as well as singing and entertaining at local establishments. The band spent time touring which wasn't exactly the environment Joe needed if he had any chance of kicking his habits of women and alcohol. Although God had finally given him a mentor, Joe was finding himself away from the Presbyterian Church more and more when Sunday came around. The temptations of being on the road with his band were too strong and Joe was succumbing more and more to the evil vices that were slowly tightening the grip on his body and soul. Once again, he came to a point of crisis and reached out helplessly for a new direction, choosing to return to the Navy for another two years of service.

By that time they had a minstrel group going so I joined the minstrel group. I was number one-in man, so I was the lowest (voice). I sang in a duet and the quartet. Of course we'd go out ... going different places to entertain. At that time, I was singing with a band and also I was on radio. We, of course, when we went out on tour, we would take our drinks with us and carry on as usual. Girls were no problem, there were a million of them seemed like. These were things that just happened from time to time. It got to be boring. Anyway we went on and on and on and my habit wasn't getting any better and things weren't going the way I wanted them to so this was when I reenlisted.

The second stint in the Navy wasn't much more for Joe than confirmation of the adage that "history has a way of repeating itself." The ray of sunshine in his otherwise hurricane-like existence was the opportunity to reinvigorate his passion for boxing. Joe was now in the prime of his boxing career much like his idol Mickey Walker was back when Joe first came into the sport. His growing list of Navy boxing accolades provided him the opportunity to test his skills with some very accomplished fighters. In fact, Joe rose through the ranks to eventually become the Junior Welterweight Champion of the Navy. His main foe at this time was a gritty Irishmen who Joe describes in the following passage...

Of course I was active in my boxing again and it seemed like things were going pretty good. We had a Junior Welterweight that I fought. He was a little redhead Irishman, tougher than nails. The first time he whipped me, and the second time I won on a foul. They called a foul then when you were hit below the belt, so I became the champion. We fought several times after that and finally he got killed so that ended that with him, but it left a sorrowful place in my heart because I really admired him and he was a good sport and a good athlete.

The Third Decade

Anyone who has ever competed at a high level in any type of athletics can understand what it means to develop a respect for one's opponent. Such was the case with Joe as he continued his boxing activities during this second two years in the Navy. He was able to develop a deep friendship with one of his staunchest foes and also continued to find himself carrying his fighting outside the ring.

> *I met another one (fighter). He was the captain's cook and he was a Phillipino. His name was David Olaldy, a great guy and we became very good friends and he was also the Junior Welterweight Champion of the Phillipines and we fought and fought and fought and I whipped him. He was the best friend that I had, we were all good friends and we would go out together and have a good time together. I never had to eat the mess that the enlisted men ate; I ate the same thing that the captain did because I was his friend. Things like these they just came along and many times we had squabbles that could have ended fatally, but thank the good Lord, they all worked out.*

It is almost unfathomable to think that Joe was now a man who had only reached his mid-twenties. Showing the same character as the teenager running track to the point of exhaustion, Joe was living as hard and fast as he could. The scenes he starred in had already provided any starving screenwriter with enough spicy material for a blockbuster Hollywood movie.

The two more years serving in the Navy and continuing to search for those elusive boundaries and a sense of purpose for life had once again proved unsuccessful. A young adult in his mid-twenties should have his life well on its way to success, but not Joe. Satan was still winning the short-term battle and Joe was continuing to fall deeper and deeper into the trappings of alcohol, rowdy behavior and a sinful lifestyle. His search for significance had fallen short. In Joe's own words he tells how futile the second years in the Navy were in his attempt to turn the corner to forgiveness and service.

These two years were about like the other four years that I'd served. It just seemed like it was one thing after another and it seemed like I was looking for something and I couldn't find exactly what I was looking for. It was out there, but I just couldn't reach it. The two years that I spent again in the Navy were about like the other four years I spent which was a drowned state of drinking and carousing around and getting into trouble and getting out of trouble. It just seemed like there was no future in any of it. So after my two years I came home.

Coming back home really didn't change things much, as a matter of fact, things were about to get to the worst they could possibly be. Joe kept his singing going, but it was tied to spending time where he shouldn't be with his propensity for the drink. On many evenings, Joe would casually saunter up to a microphone at the front of the local Moose Lodge and begin singing. This, of course, would get the attention of all the young, unattached girls there to scope out the young bachelors. The bachelors were there for the same reason, to find an unattached girl. Once this ritual had begun, it was brought to a higher level when the alcohol was put into the mix.

There was one young girl who was especially "taken" with Joe. She was a beautiful, dark-skinned, dark-haired girl of Italian decent. It seemed she gravitated to Joe and he didn't shy away from her at first. They would spend most evenings dancing and drinking the night away. Joe, however, in his own words had become "bored" with girls and just another escapade with another attractive girl wasn't appealing. He would dance, drink and talk with the girl, but that seemed to be the extent of it. She apparently wanted a relationship, but Joe had experienced the futility of these "pass in the night" encounters. He felt there must be more.

Not long after he was back home, he thought perhaps his life would finally turn around. He met a young woman named Dorothy. Their relationship started like many of his others, but quickly rose to a much higher level. Whether it was that Joe wanted a normal relationship so badly he overlooked what should have been obvious, was blinded by the constant alcohol, or for whatever reason, the relationship with Dorothy went from a casual one to one that ended in a disastrous, short-lived marriage. It's not known how long the two lived together, but it couldn't have been more than a few days the first time and then perhaps a month when Dorothy showed up on the steps of Joe's mother and stepfather's home announcing she was Joe's wife and was there to stay with her new husband.

Dorothy soon left the scene and Joe's understanding was that she was filing for a divorce of the doomed pseudo-relationship. Even though the marriage was short-lived, by the time Dorothy left she was pregnant with their child. The continuing search for a fulfilled life had just taken a sharp turn downward and Joe's answer once again was to return to the only thing he knew, escaping to the bottle. If he could just drink enough, perhaps he could escape his troubles. He did when he was "liquored up", but the fact was when he "sobered up" the problems were still there.

The child he had fathered with Dorothy also didn't disappear by sinking into an alcoholic stupor. Joe was never allowed to see his child after it was born. He really didn't even know at this time whether the child was a boy or girl. On one occasion, however, Joe thought he saw his ex-wife go by riding on an Indianapolis city bus. He saw her, she saw him and he caught a brief glimpse of his child on her lap. That would be his only connection with the child until much later in his life. Dorothy did try to involve Joe in the child's life, but only by attempting to get money from him and his family. It wasn't that Joe wanted to shirk his responsibility, in fact it was just the opposite, but Dorothy would come and go day to day, week to week based on whether or not she had squandered any and all money Joe had been able to scrape together.

Of course, this is not to say he was totally without fault in this situation. He was still drinking and had sunk to one of the lowest levels of his already tragic existence on this earth. His worldly attempts at achieving happiness and joy had all just kept making Joe feel more and more empty rather than having any true fulfillment.

It was at this lowest time of Joe's life that he relates a truly miraculous happening. Many have experienced some sort of divine intervention in their lives, but Joe's words of a life changing event sends chills down the spine of anyone who listens to the tape of his words describing such an event. Joe had been out on one of his now nearly routine binges and dragged his body home.

Of course my drinking habit was as bad as it was before so one night I came home and I was completely intoxicated. I came in and got in the front room and fell in a chair and that's where I sat. While I sat there I could here a voice say to me, "Get up and look in the mirror." Well, I'm the type of person nobody told anything to. I did what I wanted to, nobody else told me. I thought to myself, "There's no way I'm going to get up and look in that mirror." And the voice came again and said, "Get up and look in the mirror." I said, "Forget it. (emphasis) I'm not getting up." The third time the voice was very, very, very stern. It said, "I said (major emphasis) get up and look in the mirror." I got up and I looked in the mirror. What I saw wasn't a very pleasant sight. I saw something that disgusted me, turned my stomach inside out. I was looking at something that wasn't me. Then I realized that somebody had spoken to me. Who was it? Who was talking to me? Then I stopped, after I sobered up I kept thinking about it and thinking about it and I decided that there was somebody who was more interested in me than I was in myself. So I cut down on my drinking. I really almost cut it completely out. The only thing I would do was drink a bottle of beer now and then. And I decided, well that's no good either.

The Third Decade

So this someone who talked to Joe and told him to look in the mirror? Who or what was it? Without saying so directly, one could surmise Joe believed it to be a voice from above because he related that later on after the tapes were completed. Not necessarily an audible voice, but most assuredly a voice he hadn't "heard" before. This was really the time when Joe's life began to turn the corner toward a higher calling and out of the depths of despair. It didn't miraculously change in that one encounter as it does for some others, but for Joe it was a life long journey and he was still learning and serving until God chose to end his time on this earth.

Joe was also seeing his life a bit clearer and his weaknesses were apparent to him and he knew for certain that he couldn't stay in the environment where he was and hope to continue to keep the image he saw in that mirror burnt in his mind. If he stayed where he was he could find ample reasons to wash away the image with more and more alcohol. He knew he had to distance himself from all the temptations he could and try to build new and more positive memories. He relates in his own words the night he made his first of many good decisions on his journey to the waiting arms of his Holy God.

> *So I was sitting on the porch with my mother one night and I said, "I'm going to go away. I want to get away from this environment that I'm in with this bunch that I'm running with. I want to get away from them." So this was when I moved to Detroit and for three years I never touched a drop of anything. I was around it all the time, it was there if I wanted it, but I never touched it.*

Michigan was a very positive, productive time in Joe's life. He worked at the Ford Motor Company and made a very good living. He could have continued working there and had a normal, fulfilled life, but that was not in God's plan. There was more painted on the life portrait of one George Huff than he or any of his past friends and family could ever dream. He still had the passion and talent in music, but this time his efforts were much more positive. He had learned to play the accordion and in this time in Michigan he entered and won contests with his now more focused talent on this unique instrument.

During this time his singing was a source of great satisfaction. Joe joined a popular local singing group called the Bluebirds. What was interesting about this group was that Joe was the only male. It consisted of three women vocalists and Joe. He jokingly referred to himself as the "thorn among three roses." They were in demand in the Detroit area and had great fun together singing and entertaining. The passion, the entertaining, the joy was there but the alcohol was not, nor was all the negative actions and interactions that had followed Joe in his early years.

Although his life was good and he was doing well, he still felt he should probably prepare for a more stable career. It was then he decided to further his education. Although the entire thought process of why Optician school was the choice is not known, Joe did enroll in school and receive his education to be an Optician. This would ultimately lead to a long and successful career in the Optical field.

Joe was ending another decade of his life's journey. This decade ended much more positive than any phase of Joe's life before. God had entered the scene in a much more powerful and purposeful way. It was much like the life of Job when he cried out to God "enough is enough." It was now time for the prodigal son to come home to his loving Father's arms to begin his life of forgiveness and service. Just as in the biblical sense Joe was returning home, he was also returning home in the literal sense. World War II was on history's horizon as was a better life for Joe and the family he had longed for all these years. Michigan had been a very positive experience overall, but his roots in Indianapolis were calling.

CHAPTER FOUR

The Fourth Decade
1940-1950
Age 30-40

"And the God of all grace, who called you to his eternal glory in Christ, after you have suffered a little while, will himself restore you and make you strong, firm and steadfast."
1 Peter 5:10

The beginning of Joe's fourth decade of life seemed like it would be much like the other three that preceded it. He was ready to return home after relatively successful years in Michigan, but still had not found that peace or place in life he so longed for. The power of alcohol for those years had been controlled to the point of no drinking at all until just shortly before his return to Indiana. For what reason no one knows, Joe was lead back to drinking beer by one of his buddies at Ford. Joe's own words let us know how this event occurred.

> *...for three years I never touched a drop of anything. I was around it all the time, it was there if I wanted it, but I never touched it. Then I was riding with a fella, I was working at Ford and I was riding with him. He would stop at the tavern every night to get a glass of beer. He would always ask me if I would take one and I kept saying "no" and finally one night, it was real hot weather and he said, "Go ahead, it will cool you off." So I drank a glass of beer with him and then I started drinking beer.*

Joe's return to Indiana was a bit different than he had imagined. Even though he had furthered his education, stopped drinking so much and had decided he was tired of "carousing" with the ladies, the idea that his life was going to be much better was just that, an idea. He came back to no job, and Arthur and Georgia had moved away from the city. He had nowhere else to live, so he had to move in with them. Here was a man thirty years old with no visible means of support, no relationships except his failed one with his first wife, Dorothy, living in an unstable world on the brink of war. He was old enough not to have to worry about another stint in the Navy, but not stable enough to take advantage of the education he had gained in Michigan. It was as if thrown back into the "old" lifestyle and surroundings, he reverted quickly to the default settings of failure and frustration set in his early years.

For the first few months back in Indiana, Joe's dreams and aspirations remained, but those hopes and dreams evaporated as quickly as fog on a summer morning. With no job and many of his old friends having moved on to another station of life, Joe was swimming in a whirlpool of desperation. God was still there, working on Joe, but at this time in his new journey toward service the era of forgiveness had begun without Joe really even knowing it. It is not always a flash of light or some catastrophic event that causes the revelations in life, but Joe's was as real as the invasion of Pearl Harbor and as long lasting as the faces on Mount Rushmore that were finished in 1941.

As a matter of fact, the image of the Japanese invading Pearl Harbor, swiftness of the attack and the long lasting ramifications of it are much like what happened to Joe shortly after his return to Indiana in his relationship to his future wife Mary Burnell. Joe had decided women were not to be a part of his life. He had so many cursory relationships with women they had lost any semblance of meaning. In Joe's words he explains his feelings.

> *After spending five years there and working at Ford and doing things that probably I shouldn't do, running with the girls again which was getting boring...*
>
> *Well, in the meantime, I'd given up girls. I'd had my fill of all of them; I didn't want any part of them.*

The Fourth Decade

The last thing Joe wanted at this time was anything to do with women. He was still trying to get his life together, find a job and get out of Georgia and Arthur's home that was now even more crowded with new half-sisters who had been born. So when his friend Harry came to ask him to go on a double date, Joe's response was a resounding, "NO!!" It was Joe's plan to stay away from women but God had other plans. After much coaching and prodding, Joe finally agreed to be the token fourth wheel on this double date he knew would go nowhere. Where Joe thought this date would come to nothing just as all his other dates had, God had plans for an initial meeting with his "helpmate" to begin a journey together that would ultimately last until his death.

The evening started out a bit differently than others Joe had been accustomed to in his eventful life. This one started and ended without the influence of alcohol at all. It was a meeting of several friends gathered together just to have fun. Mary, Joe's date, describes the evening in the exact same terms as did Joe. The two didn't arrive together, and weren't even introduced formally at the beginning of the evening. The men basically hung outside while the girls were in the house playing the game Carom. This is a game similar to pool with small, round wooden circles instead of pool balls and the object of the game was to take a black carom and flip it into your color carom and send the colored one into one of the four pockets located at each corner of the board.

Mary remembers that night that as she was playing carom, when she would get one of her caroms into the pocket she would let out a loud scream and laugh about her accomplishment. The memories Joe shares are exactly the same as Mary's even after more than sixty years passed. It should be no surprise to anyone then, that the night Joe and Mary met was a life changing experience for both. Joe recounts that first meeting with the young Mary in his own words.

I was standing out front talking to some of the fellas, and we were just standing there talking and I heard somebody laughing. I looked in and I saw a girl. I asked him, "Who's that?" He said, "That's your date." And I said, "Oh." (emphasis)

To say that Joe and Mary "hit it off" that first night would be a rather large understatement. It was 1941, the war had just begun in earnest, but the atomic bomb that would be unleashed four years later in Japan had already been unleashed in both Joe and Mary's hearts. The picture of love at first sight was in play on this double date night. With Joe so adamantly not wanting to attend, and Mary with a boyfriend somewhere else, who would have thought God would have placed these two seemingly different people together at this party and ultimately for the rest of Joe's life? With Joe's life to this point being so tragic and traumatic, God was beginning to heal the wounds of a hard life and begin Joe's journey of forgiveness on the road to service with Mary at his side.

All other relationships with women to this point had been short lived and for all the wrong reasons. This relationship, although nowhere near what people would think of as conventional, was to be different in ways other than just on the surface. It would be a deep, caring, loving commitment between man and woman just as God had designed it.

At the beginning of the evening, Joe didn't want to be there and wanted to go home. By the end of the evening Joe wanted to be with Mary and wanted to escort her home so they would have more time to talk. That night brought the beginning of a whirlwind romance that took two seemingly mismatched people from not knowing one another to marriage in a short time period. Although Joe had not wanted to go with his friend Harry to the party, he now didn't want to go back home with him. By evening's end Joe and Mary had met, talked, and had already begun to build a relationship with one another. Joe relates the way the night ended.

> *So later on in the evening I met her and she and I got along very, very well together so I took her home and I asked her for another date and she said "yes."*

Despite all of Joe's recent attempts to put the opposite gender out of his mind and, more importantly, out of his lifestyle, the successful double date with Mary was all he could think about. It was an extremely frustrating feeling not being able to put her aside and focus on his newly attained independence and self-control. But the evening was so unlike any other he had ever experienced with any other woman. There hadn't been the normal out of control drinking, and general seediness that was characteristic of most of the parties Joe attended. Anyone who has ever fallen in love can understand what Joe was going through at this time. His heart was leading the way and his mind was following like a dutiful understudy.

The budding relationship between Mary and Joe was special and unique from the very start. In the 21st century's view of dating and relationships, Joe and Mary would not be given a chance. If they were placed on one of today's reality TV dating shows, no one in the viewing audience or answering an Internet poll would even think about voting for the two to become a couple. The odds of a blind double date ever working are numbers that a Vegas "bookie" would take any day.

From a modern, materialistic point of view, Joe did not come off as the most eligible bachelor. He was thirty-one years old owning nothing more than the clothes on his back, had no car and was living with his parents. He also had no defined career path. In fact he didn't even have a job. An occupation was necessary since his family name obviously carried with it no special endowment. Another factor that should have prevented the two from becoming an item was the fact that Joe was nearly twice as old as Mary. When they met, he was thirty-one and she was only seventeen. Maybe this was a blessing in disguise. It probably helped Mary see all the wonderful qualities of Joe and not the social stigmas that he carried with him.

As if this wasn't enough, the final roadblock that the two faced was that Mary was already engaged at the time despite her young age. Of course this was perfect for Joe's personality because once he realized he was attracted to Mary, his competitive nature spurred him on to be her knight in shining armor and take her away from his foe. Joe wasn't one to shy away from a good fight be it literal or figurative so what would have been a problem for most, turned into a quest for him.

God was definitely orchestrating the whole process of Joe and Mary meeting and beginning their courtship. Not that they were even aware of it at the time because they weren't, but God was conducting them through all these social barriers with the same ease and gracefulness as a maestro maneuvering his baton through the rough spots of a complex symphonic score. They were meant to be together and it wouldn't take long for that realization to be revealed to both of them.

The benefit of Joe's lack of focus in his life and his transient lifestyle at this time was his freedom to come and go. He didn't have the normal distractions and busyness of life standing in the way of romance like we see so often with thirty-year-olds today who are on the fast track struggling to achieve the coveted prizes of fame and wealth. Without a steady job to distract him, his work became the quest to see Mary every day and in his usual steadfast way, that was exactly what he did. She was working as a sort of nanny for a family in the city caring for a young boy and maintaining the house. She was paid five dollars per week for her efforts, which was a fair wage for the time considering she was also getting room and board, but by no means the kind of money to get excited about.

Every night for the next seven months, Joe would take the bus from the outskirts of town where he lived with his parents to see Mary at the house where she was living and working. He would stay with her until the last bus left town. With little money between them this time together was very short on frills, but very high in quality. The only entertainment they afforded themselves was walking to the movies every Wednesday night.

Mary had broken off her prior engagement early into the new relationship with Joe and their love for each other grew very quickly. They knew that a wedding was on the horizon, but as was the case throughout Joe's life, it couldn't come easily. Joe briefly describes the engagement in the following words:

Well, at the time she (Mary) was engaged and the fella she was engaged to wasn't much of a fella I guess because she gave him his ring back and started going with me. So one day I went down and I bought an engagement ring and a wedding band. That night I took it out and I put it on her finger. She had to run down the street and show this girlfriend of hers, the one that was at the party, and she looked at it and she said to me, "Anytime she gives it back I'll take it." But thank the good Lord she never gave it back.

After their engagement while applying for their marriage license, Joe's Aunt who worked at the local courthouse, discovered that the divorce from Dorothy had never been finalized. Joe had to place a notice in the paper and wait for ten days to see if Dorothy would contest it before he could cross this final hurdle and be legally cleared to marry again. They had met in March of 1941 and by October 15th of the same year Joe and Mary were wed in Greenwood, IN and began a life together that would last for fifty-six years.

Of course there was no big house at the end of the block and no white picket fence awaited the newlyweds. Instead, Mary had arranged with her employer for Joe to move in and live with them as part of her compensation. After being married only a week and feeling the new responsibility of having a wife, God pointed Joe in the direction of Kernel's, a full-service Optical business located in the heart of downtown Indianapolis just off Monument Circle. Kernel's was a large, thriving business. Several doctors practiced there and all of the eyewear that was prescribed for the patients was manufactured on site. Joe was hired and for the first time in his life, had the prospects of financial stability within his grasp. He was a model employee and soon developed a passion for his work.

The work environment was perfectly suited for Joe's personality and was strikingly similar to the type of work that characterized his first job at the barbershop. The front of Kernel's was very attractive and modern for the day. The patient area and doctor's offices were well appointed and bright from the light streaming in all the windows. Being situated downtown, the office had an exciting buzz about it and smelled of progress and affluence. This, however, was not the part of the business where Joe labored. Much like he did as a young boy serving the dirty railroaders in the back of the shop, Joe once again found himself toiling out of the eyesight of the customers.

To get to his work area, you had to go down a long hallway that quickly became dark and damp and led toward the back of the building. The big windows looking out over the city streets and the painted walls of the Doctor's offices decorated with modern artwork and colorful accents, was exchanged for the windowless brick walls and dark recesses of the back room of the building where the eyeglasses were made by hand. This was a place the patients never saw, nor did most of the doctors for that matter. This didn't bother Joe, however. He was delighted for the opportunity to do something that interested him and to receive the extra benefit of earning a wage as a result. His optical schooling while living in Michigan a few years earlier had allowed him this chance at stability. The closed space of the small, back room of Kernel's now served as the first real positive boundary in Joe's tumultuous life and he wasn't going to let it slip away. In a prophetic sort of way, Joe's service of crafting eyeglasses was now providing the means for others to see and experience life more clearly, something that Joe would continue doing until his last days.

While the job provided some hope for the new couple, they couldn't immediately escape the challenges that were being presented. Just a few short weeks into their marriage, the lady who Mary worked for decided to quit her job as a nurse and stay home with her son. This obviously left Mary without work and consequently left her and Joe without a place to live. Just as there were many reasons why the two should never have gotten married, this forced move so early in their relationship would be the start of many events over the next several years that would make it difficult for them to stay together without the grace of God in their lives.

With no place to live, a new wife, job, and responsibilities Joe once again seemed crushed with the weight of life. As God continued to work on Joe and place him farther down on his road to service through the time of forgiveness He placed another interloper to help in the process. Joe's Uncle Fred called to solve the dilemma. Fred informed Joe and Mary that Grandma Huff (Jeannie), Guy's mother, would take the newlyweds in if Mary would agree to do the housework and cooking. Jeannie Huff was seventy-six when the move occurred. The hope of a house together was soon replaced by a house divided when the news came that Mary was now with child.

Grandma Huff was okay with the two living with her and helping in the day-to-day tasks, but a newborn was not a part of her deal with the two. It did not help either, that Joe had more and more often disappeared in the evenings to the local bar to share stories and drink with his buddies. This was not as severe as in the past, but still at a level to cause problems with his grandmother and Mary. Mary, after all, was not a direct family member and had little in common with the seventy-six-year-old Jeannie. Mary was still only seventeen and the generational differences were as wide as the chasm of the Grand Canyon, which was something Joe wanted to see sometime in his life. But this chasm between his grandmother and his young wife was something he wanted to escape and he did so at the local bar.

Those first few months were traumatic, but it got even worse after the baby was born. For whatever reasons, probably just to escape the new responsibilities, the night young George W. Huff, Jr. came to join the family, Joe reverted to his escape hatch of the bottle. When the baby arrived, Joe was not to be found on the scene. This situation underscored the fact that Joe still had a long way to travel in his journey. Mary was very hurt and disillusioned at this recent setback. To hear the story related after so many years the hurt can still be heard resonating in her voice. The love of her life, the leader of her family, the father of her son, not even being at the hospital when the child came was devastating for the young seventeen-year-old girl. If it had not been for the fact that Mary herself had come from such a traumatic childhood, it could have been a deal breaker and Mary could have told Joe to "take a hike", but she had been through tougher times than this and she was committed to making this marriage work. God had given Joe a mate who would help bring that structure to his life and hold him accountable for his actions in order to keep him directed toward what God ultimately had in store for him.

To emphasize Joe's path had begun to be more positive was his "stepping up to the plate" to take responsibility for the financial implications of George Jr.'s birth. It should go without saying that no money was available for health insurance, so the birth and the stay in the hospital had to be paid for in some other manner. When Joe finally did get to the hospital to visit Mary and the baby, he began to discuss with his young bride how they would meet the obligation of payment. He had thought it through and saw no way other than going to his boss, Dr. Joe Kernel, and asking for a loan. He was surprised by his young wife's reaction. Rather than saying yes, that was their only option, she told Joe to go to the house and look in her sock drawer. There he was to find a black sock with money in it. Mary, much unlike Joe, had thought ahead and had been putting the change she had received back from her grocery shopping trips in the sock. She really had no idea how much was there, but it could off set at least a part of the bill they would be facing.

In God's most powerful and faithful way, when Joe found the money and counted it, there was just enough to pay the entire bill. Was this just a coincidence or a gift from God who was forgiving and preparing His prodigal son for future service?

The joy of God's provision was short lived with the young couple and the new bouncing baby boy. Upon coming back to the home of Jeannie, she quickly let the new expanded family know they were no longer welcome in her home. One can come to a quick conclusion this was a "heartless" old woman who didn't care about family, but the realization is this was a seventy-six-year-old woman who had taken in a needy couple when she could have easily denied the request from the outset. She didn't however, and the few months she had allowed them to stay had at least let Mary accumulate the money to pay the bill for George Jr.'s (Billy) birth. God had provided for Joe and Mary and now Billy for the short term and would do so once again as He was already way ahead of Joe and had prepared the next place to live. One request and Georgia and Arthur's home was opened to the newly expanded family.

Again though there was another move for the new Huff family, each change and each page of life that was lived seemed to become more and more positive and productive in the continual shaping of one Joe Huff. When looking at Joe's life in this time period, it would be easy to fall into the false sense this was just the same tragic event happening over and over again. The difference at this time in these transition years is the evidence of God shaping and honing Joe for the future. He was beginning to have consistency in other areas of his life even though his move from one house to another seemed to continue. His job was stable and he was beginning to see the importance of his work and providing for his family.

In the quiet solitude of his small, dark optician's work area, Joe began to spend time reflecting and thinking about his life and what God might have in store for him and his family. As Joe patiently shaped the glass lenses for Kernel, God was patiently doing the same to Joe's character for the task yet to come in helping shape people's lives. The image of Joe creating glasses for people of all ages to see clearer, cannot be lost as a comparison of his creating a church environment and living a life where others could see Christ through him and his preaching. Joe didn't foresee how God was going to use him just as Kernel's customers didn't see clearly through less than perfect eyes. While Joe used the abrasives of sand and gravel to polish and refine the glass lenses, God was using and had used the sand and gravel of the tough life Joe had lived and was continuing to live to refine him for the service portion of his life's journey.

One specific way God continued to use Joe's past to help shape him for his future was bringing images and experiences to his mind on a nearly daily basis. As Joe would exit the bus on his way to his place of solitude in the recesses of Kernel Optical, he would pass by young men and women standing on the corner or walking the streets of downtown Indianapolis who seemed to have no direction and no destination. God was putting these images in front of Joe to remind him of where he had once been and that there should be no return to those fruitless, faithless, wasted days. In his younger years, Joe had been dubbed the "Drugstore Cowboy" by his loving little sister, Charlotte. Now as Joe passed by young men who had taken over his place as the "Drugstore Cowboys" of new, he found himself not longing for that life at all, but longing for continued forgiveness and direction from God.

There was quickly approaching another move for the relatively new family, but this was a move toward a more positive life. Mary had again been saving and planning to be able to once and for all be in a home of their own. Not to discount the gratefulness both she and Joe felt for being allowed to live in Georgia and Arthur's home, but the fact was God was making it abundantly clear it was time to continue the growth in the faithfulness and dedication to a life with Christ in the center.

As D-Day approached in the European theatre of WWII,

the D-Day (Departure of Dependents) was also approaching for Arthur and Georgia. The new family of Joe, Mary and Billy was about to embark on a new chapter of life. A chapter of life they had never been able to experience before; that of living alone in their own home as a nuclear family. Joe's new found steadfastness and dedication to his job and family had allowed this move to be possible. That is not to say they had it all together yet, but at least they were on their way to independence as a family. For the first years of their marriage they had relied on family to provide, now they were beginning to understand their faith and dependence had to be on one another, but more importantly on God.

It was 1943 and the move to the home on Rawls Avenue brought about an exciting new way of living for Joe, Mary and young Billy. It signaled the first time that they were able to truly say they were on their own surviving without the charity of others. In contrast to the turmoil of a nation at war, God was now providing a time of relative peace and normality for Joe. It was as if God gave Joe a "time-out" at this point in his life, a time to sort of let some grass grow under his feet. It was also an opportunity to experience the blessing of a day-to-day existence with things being more the same instead of the constant change that he was used to enduring.

To someone else who had not gone through the same things as Joe, this time in his life could have seemed dull and stagnant, yet to Joe it was just the opposite. The consistency of a good, steady job, a marriage that was strengthening by the day and the satisfaction of providing for his family was precisely what Joe needed.

The house on Rawls Avenue was nothing special even to the average person. It was located on the near-eastside of Indianapolis just a stone's throw away from Washington Street, also called State Road 40 which has been chronicled in many history books as the Old National Road used by so many in the westward movement as they passed through the "Crossroads of

America." The house was a single-story duplex that had been a light gray color and was in need of a fresh coat of paint. It was a metaphor of the life Joe and Mary had experienced to this point. Stark, small, void of furniture and in need of repair, it was just like their lives. Just as they systematically worked together to furnish the house over time, their lives were, over time, converted to a life of dedication and love for one another, there soon-to-be larger family and most importantly their love and service to the Lord.

The stability that God was providing Joe allowed him to gain more and more momentum on the road to maximizing his full potential. The concept of success breeding success was materializing in Joe's life through the choices he was now making. The snowball effect was working for him instead of against him. The same person who as a young boy continually found himself on the wrong side of the fence was now beginning to experience the freedom and rewards that came from being on the right side.

Joe had come far enough along in his life that he began filling his spare time serving his community as an Auxiliary Police Officer. He had spent much of his first three decades on the fringe of the law many times just a blink of the eye away from being removed from society. Now, however, he was contributing positively to society by protecting others from the same kinds of trouble that used to reach out and grab him over and over again. His role in the Auxiliary Police provided another opportunity to see the life he came from in the eyes and actions of those he was now helping.

God's forgiveness and grace could also be seen in the smaller, day-to-day things of life for Joe and his family. On one such occasion, Mary traveled to the grocery store to get, among other things, some items Joe needed for the lunch he carried to work each day. It was the winter of 1944 and there was a wet snow on the ground. The walk back from the store was long enough that Mary decided to stop for a moment to rest. The sidewalk had been cleared of most of the snow and appeared clean enough to set the two bags of groceries down to give her arms some much needed relief. When she went to pick up the bags and continue on her way, the bottoms tore away and the hard-earned food spilled out on the wet ground. With no other option available, she decided to make the long walk home and fetch a sturdier container for the items. Anxiety and regret crept in as she realized the chances were small that the groceries would still be there when she returned because of the food rationing in place due to World War II. Despite things being better than in the past, this sort of an episode was not something the family budget would be able to withstand. Much to her surprise and excitement, however, when she returned to the scene all the food was there exactly as she had left it. In this simple occurrence of life, Joe and his family were able to experience another dose of God's grace and provision.

The items Mary brought back from the grocery store that day did more than just symbolize God's grace they also symbolized an emerging characteristic of Joe. He was a creature of habit, so much so that he carried the same items in his work lunch every day for as long as anyone can remember. His lunch consisted of a baloney sandwich, an orange, four Fig Newtons and a thermos of cold coffee. One of the comforting things about a relationship with God is that His Word says He is the same yesterday, today and tomorrow. God is the Rock amidst all the trials and turmoil that life brings. God's unchanging, unfailing ways and love provides the refuge needed as life races past. It seemed that Joe had already discovered this concept in his life even though his relationship to God was only in its infancy.

The nation was on the brink of fast-paced change with the invention of the first computer in 1945, and Chuck Yeager made his mark by breaking the sound barrier just a short time later. Even though the pace of life was speeding up all around him, Joe was beginning to see the advantages of a simple life free from a lot of distractions and change, which was illustrated in the ordinary event of opening his lunch box every day in his cozy, peaceful spot at the back of Kernel's Optical Company.

Joe's development and steadfastness was evident in many phases of his life. He was becoming a creature of habit and consistency. The habits he was developing were the good ones and many of the old ones were gone or leaving his life in a systematic manner. Although at this time still smoking and drinking an occasional bottle of beer, it was secondary to his family and his growth. A real example of this was when his second child, Betty Jean, was born on March 1, 1945. Unlike when Billy was born, Joe was there by Mary's side enjoying the new gift God had given them. This new life was welcomed into the family with joy and anticipation and her coming home was a welcomed event unlike when Billy came to Grandma Huff's. This was in large part to the home Joe and Mary were building and the continued forgiveness they were experiencing in their walk toward a life centered on God. Just as their little home on Rawls Avenue was filling up with furniture and family, Joe and Mary's lives were being filled with love and dedication to each other.

After two short years, another bundle of joy came unexpectedly into the Huff family. Carol Ann was born on February 14, 1947. She added to the filling of the family and home in both a figurative and literal sense. It was as if God had placed the final piece needed to complete the family unit.

Although Mary had not been raised by parents who thought it important to attend church, Joe had the church in his background. He realized how important it was and even though he was still working on ridding himself of the last vestiges of his old habits, he knew the place his family needed to be was in church. Unlike his earlier church experiences where he went because he was told to or because he wanted to socialize with his gang buddies and be close to a pastor he cared about, he wanted to be in church now because he knew it was what he should do. The last thing Joe wanted was his children and wife suffering what he had suffered while growing up. God was not only filling the house on Rawls with furniture and family, he was filling it up with a thirst for the Word and hope for a better tomorrow through a life lived in God's will.

Joe began taking his family to a church on Downey Avenue just a few blocks from the small house on Rawls. It was close enough for them to walk since there was still no money for a car. Yes, things were much better for Joe and Mary, but not yet had they escaped the bondage of lower class society in a material sense. They had, however, moved a long way in escaping this bondage in the spiritual sense. During this decade of transition, God had begun to slowly take Joe from His protection to His forgiveness and had begun to form the Huff family and specifically its leader, Joe, into the servant he was to become. Just as it was not easy for Joe to make those glasses at Kernel's quickly and without great painstaking work, it was the same painstaking, patient sharpening of Joe's faith God began in earnest through this decade of Joe's thirties to forties.

In the late 1940's the Polaroid Instamatic Camera was invented and placed on the market. For the first time a person could take a picture and within one minute it was developed and ready for viewing. Not so with the life of Joe. Looking at old snapshots of Joe's life and looking at snapshots taken by the new Polaroid, one would see great differences, but God was not done working yet. There would be many more changes and the picture of Joe's life would become more and more beautiful year after year until his death. In the early snapshots Joe would be at the center with his mustache, his smirk on his face and an "I got the world by the tail" attitude hiding the hurt and pain the camera could not penetrate. Now, in the late 1940's the picture would have Joe more in the background, quietly working, serving and listening, as God became more the centerpiece of the portrait.

Joe's own words emphasize what was occurring in his life at this time. What an amazing change God was already making!

So here I realized that another thing was taking place in my life, a new environment, because we got married. And then we had a son. Then we had two daughters. Then the great change came because my life changed completely around. I had responsibilities that I had to take care of and I had somebody who would work with me instead of against me. And I know deep in my heart that God had planned this from the beginning… We raised our children in church. We took them. We didn't send them by themselves, we took them and we raised them the way that God wanted us to raise them.

It was the end of another decade of Joe's life, but what a great decade it was! Where in the past most things were negative; this decade was much like March in Indiana is said to be, it came in like a lion and went out like a lamb. God had faithfully protected Joe in the first thirty years of his life and now had him firmly on the road of forgiveness and fullness of life. He began the decade with nothing and ended the decade with what most people only dream of… a great family, wife, job and a deepening faith in God. Another move was in the near future, but again this would be a positive one for the family of Joe Huff.

CHAPTER FIVE

The Fifth Decade
1950-1960
Age 40-50

"Do not conform any longer to the pattern of this world, but be transformed by the renewing of your mind. Then you will be able to test and approve what God's will is-his good, pleasing and perfect will."
Romans 12:2

In 1950 the Korean War had begun and many young men were going off to war and families were being separated. Joe and his family were on the move too, not being split apart, but in a sense they were being sent to a foreign atmosphere. Joe and Mary had decided it was time to move from the city into a more rural setting. On the surface it may not appear like a drastic change, but to the young Huff family this move was significant. It was a move away from the city and also the beginning of going away from many of the bad memories and habits that had been adding up over the first forty years of Joe's life. State Road 421 would be the new address of Joe, Mary, Billy, Betty and Carol Huff.

This move entailed many changes in addition to just the physical move from city life to a more rural life. Although the relatively new family was still living in a rented home, it was now a home away from the urban life Joe had experienced. Because of the move, city transportation was no longer available. In the past Joe had always used the bus to get to and from Kernel's Optical and the family had walked to their church on Downy Avenue, but the move to State Road 421 would cause the young couple to have to purchase a car. The car was important so Joe could get back and forth to work, but also very important to provide a way to continue to raise the family in the church. Their rural location made it no longer possible to walk to worship, but the new car and the commitment of Joe and Mary allowed them to continue their growth and discipline of a faith-based family.

Joe had not owned a car since the one his father had left him at his death and that vehicle had long sense been retired from service. Joe's first family car was a Model "A" Ford, not much different than his first. This was an old car for that time, but nonetheless a new page in the life of Joe. Now he was not only a family man, but also began having more and more responsibilities and financial obligations that had to be met.

In the past Joe would most likely have run to the bottle or some other escape to get away from those issues, but now as God's continuing forgiveness kept coming into his life more and more, Joe's steadfast dedication to his family and fulfilling his responsibilities overrode any feelings of his needing to escape. In fact it was about this time that Joe relates how God made it clear the drinking couldn't just be cut down as he had already done, but needed to be purged completely from his life.

Joe had quit going to bars and spending money, but he would still come home after work and drink an occasional beer. Because of Joe's personal struggle with alcohol, God rid him of the desire for it. Listening to Joe's words one gets the realization of how powerful and direct our Holy Father can be. In Joe's early life his earthly father, Guy, had taken him to the shed and punished him for actions he felt were inappropriate. Joe was afraid of Guy and the punishment seemed not to work well, because it was not accompanied by any show of love.

Not so, with God's discipline of Joe and his drinking. God knew what was best for Joe and his family so when Joe didn't stop the use of alcohol, God stepped into the picture in a very real way and took care of the problem. Joe couldn't solve the dilemma, but God could and did. In Joe's own words he tells us how God took away a demon that had been following him for most of the years of his life and did so as quickly as sun can appear after a spring storm.

The Fifth Decade

It seems strange that the Lord has his ways of taking things away that we don't need. I would go home of an evening and I would drink beer and it was fine until a time came that I drank one and it made me sick, deathly sick. I had to go to bed. I couldn't even hold my head up. So I thought, perhaps that I needed to change and buy another brand which I did, but the same thing happened. I thought well perhaps maybe I shouldn't drink bottled beer, maybe I should drink canned beer. So I bought that and then the same thing happened. So bought a different brand again and the same thing happened. I thought to myself, "Well this is foolishness. If it's going to make me sick I'm not going to drink it." So I quit, not realizing that it was the Lord's work not mine.

At this time in history, the early 1950's, a new innovation came along, the credit card. Joe and his family didn't have a credit card, but they had managed to build up some debt that was beginning to take its toll. Joe, even though in a stable work environment, was not bringing home much money and with the additional cost of the car, gasoline and the bigger home in the country, the meager dollars earned just did not go as far. To compensate for extra dollars needed, the couple decided that perhaps Mary could go to work for a short time to supplement the income until some of the debts were paid off and Joe could get a raise. In their thinking this would be an arrangement that would only last a few weeks. Mary would work nights and be with the children in the days while Joe would play "Mr. Mom" at night.

Some men of this era may have thought it an imposition or unfair to come home after a hard day of work and then care for three small children, but Joe basked in the opportunity to spend time with his kids. His love and devotion to his family was evident in the joy he showed by being given the opportunity to nurture his children. In today's society, families realize the importance and have totally accepted fathers taking on more of the nurturing role; Joe was just way ahead of his time. As God was nurturing and caring for Joe preparing him for his life of service, Joe was doing the same for his three small children.

The house on State Road 421 was a very modest one by most standards, but to Joe and his family the additional cost of rent bought them a significant improvement in living conditions from what they had in the city. The house was not what one would consider being out in the country but it was definitely more rural than any other location the family had lived in before. In modern terms, the Huffs now lived in the suburbs although in 1950, there weren't the miles of strip malls, billboards and restaurants that define the suburban landscape of the 21st century. Away from the hustle and bustle of the city that had defined the forty years of Joe's life thus far, he now had the blessing of experiencing life at a slower pace and had fewer distractions to deal with once he had completed his work for the day.

The house, which was protected by white-tiled siding, did not sit far off the road and a small covered porch provided a welcoming feel to any visitor who might come calling. A short drive extended along the right side of the house from the road where there was a side entrance into the kitchen in the back of the main level. If entering the front of the home from the porch, one found a small, but cozy living room with a smaller adjoining family room that faced to the rear of the property. The fourth room on the main floor was the main bedroom in the front right corner. The first level was very functional despite the fact that no room was larger than 10 ft by 12 ft. One of the distinguishing characteristics of this humble abode was the stairway located in the kitchen. Two small bedrooms were upstairs, one in the front where Billy slept along with a sixteen year old family member of Mary's who was living there and one in the rear which served as the bedroom for the two girls, Betty and Carol. The window in the upstairs front bedroom could be opened out onto the roof of the porch, which the girls used as a favorite place to play.

With no other rooms in the house to describe, it is appropriate to point out that despite the improved living conditions, the Huff family found themselves in a home that did not have a bathroom nor did it have any internal running water. A small building out to the right of the house served as the restroom and a large metal washtub still provided the only means for bathing and doing wash.

Betty and Carol were both very young at this time, which made the task of going to the outhouse at night very unpleasant if not downright scary and near impossible in the winter. Joe handled this dilemma with an unselfish act that showed his children how much he loved them. A round porcelain pot was normally used as the temporary bathroom inside the house. For Joe, the picture of his little girls having to rise from bed and make their way downstairs in the cold, dark middle of night just didn't seem right. So, he would carry the pot upstairs at bedtime and position it close to their room so they could go to the bathroom and quickly return to the warmth and safety of their beds.

Of course, this made the task of emptying the pot in the morning much more perilous and uncomfortable for Joe. In fact, on one occasion, as he was bringing the pot downstairs he stumbled causing all the contents to spill out over the floor and unfortunately on him too. An event like this would try the patience of even the most even-tempered individual, but to Joe it was merely a chance to stop and have a good, hearty laugh at himself. He didn't lash out at the girls for "causing" his situation and he didn't launch into a string of foul language; he just laughed and took everything in stride, because he was serving the ones he loved.

His part time role as "Mr. Mom" which included providing for his girls' dance lessons and taking his son to accordion lessons, along with the peace that came from their surroundings at this time allowed Joe to start to understand just how far God's forgiveness of his past had brought him. He was beginning to see the pieces of the puzzle come together and through the eyes of his wife and children, Joe was realizing that God was giving him all the desires of his heart.

His children bore a striking similarity to him and his siblings. His oldest was a boy, just as Joe was the oldest in his family. His middle child, Betty, as a baby reminded him of the few pictures the family treasured of Edna. Finally, his youngest daughter, Carol brought to mind his sister Charlotte. Joe watched his young family growing up and beginning to create their own memories and relationships.

To his credit, Joe was doing his part to help the equation too. Any person who goes through the exercise of tracing his or her family roots can see the effects of past generations on the current one. The links to Joe's past were tainted with poverty, tragedy and loneliness but he was now taking it upon himself to chart a new course for his family. He was forging a new direction that would have a lasting impact for generations to follow.

A major scientific breakthrough occurred in 1953 with the discovery of DNA. Ironically, genetics played a part in a significant occurrence in Joe's life in the very same year. It was like any other day of work. Joe was meticulously going about his duties in the back of the downtown optical building. As he was working, Joe heard his name called from the hallway between the front of the store and the back room where he was located. The male voice called out informing Joe that there was a young lady in the front of the store asking for him. A young lady, Joe must have thought? The idea of a young lady coming to his place of employment unannounced and interrupting his work must have tossed his mind into a spontaneous flurry of activity. Maybe twenty years ago this would have made sense. But Joe was forty-three years old with a wife and three young children. Something was out of place for this to be happening at this point in his life. With part curiosity and part anxiety, Joe put down the set of glasses he was working on and made his way to the front of the building, a place where he rarely had occasion to show himself. As he emerged through the doorframe and into the waiting area he saw her standing there. The image of the young woman immediately sparked a feeling inside him that he couldn't understand nor describe. Her features seemed familiar although he was certain they had never met. She was a few inches shorter than Joe with straight, black hair and high cheekbones. She was a very attractive woman who Joe was about to discover was eighteen years old.

"Are you George Huff?" she asked.

Joe responded affirmatively, still racing through the Rolodex in his mind in an attempt to place whom this person was and how she knew him and where he worked. Then after what must have seemed like an eternity, the odd feeling that was inside of him was instantly explained.

"I'm your daughter," she said.

It all made sense now although Joe must have been coming up with more questions than answers as a result of this startling development. Of course he knew of her and had a brief glimpse of her through the window of a bus being held in the arms of her mother as they traveled past him in the city. But that was an entirely different picture than the scene now playing out before him. While not all of the details of that day are known, what is certain is the fact that Joe and his estranged daughter made an instant connection to one another. From that moment on they would remain a part of each other's lives.

What an amazing lesson this was for Joe at this point in his life and an enduring lesson for anyone today. While this phase of Joe's life was defined by God's forgiveness of the sins of his past, it is also a striking reminder that the consequences of sin are real despite God's grace. There was no DNA test required in the lobby of Kernel Optical that day. The young adult woman who had so dramatically re-entered Joe's life was the undeniable physical representation of the careless forays of his past. He was now forced to confront his earlier years and he did so with all the honesty and integrity that exemplified who Joe was as a person. He accepted this woman and did not turn his back on her or deny that he was responsible for bringing her into the world. Over the course of the next several years before she moved out

West, Joe took an active role in her life. He was there walking her down the aisle at her wedding. He shared her joy as she gave birth to his first two grandchildren. The two also spent many times reminiscing about the years of her life that they had spent away from one another.

The time Joe spent with his young adult daughter did not compromise the responsibilities to his nuclear family. Joe tried to be a model father to his three young children in every way. He cherished his time with them. He was fun-loving, playful and wonderfully ornery. Most surprising of all, was his gentleness as a father. The barrel-chested, square-jawed boxer who made a name for himself as a tough, gritty fighter was to his children a very approachable, sweet and caring man. As evidence of his caring nature, he continued whenever possible to look for ways to better their lives. Another move taking Joe one step further away from his past was soon to occur.

In 1954 Joe and his family made this move. This time it was to a very rural setting in eastern Boone County, Indiana. They moved to a small farm on a gravel road. It was a small house without many amenities. The most significant difference from this move and all the others, however, was that this house was purchased and not rented. It sat on nine acres of land with a barn, garage and huge, mature trees surrounding the house. Joe's search to distance himself from the city and the unpleasant memories of his youth had now been fully realized with his transition from the "Drugstore Cowboy" to the "Gentleman Farmer."

With this purchase of the home and the mortgage that went with it, Mary's temporary job became a permanent one. The two had decided the life they wanted to live for themselves and for their children was worth the sacrifice of both working to pay the bills. Without someone like Joe with the love and dedication for his kids, this arrangement would probably not have worked. When Mary began working outside the home, the family structure remained firm. In fact, it gave Joe the opportunity to continue to be an influential part of his children's lives and strengthened the family unit instead of weakening it in any way.

The Fifth Decade

The small, two story, white, frame house sat in the front of the property. Three large weeping willow trees adorned the front yard. One sat at the side of the gravel drive just at the right front of the acre or so where the buildings were placed. The garage was large enough for two cars, but had no doors and was more of a carport type structure than a true garage. The barn had once supported a larger farming operation; but for many years had been sparingly used and let deteriorate to a point where much renovation would not have been a wise use of the family's meager earnings. It was, however, still useable and Joe did manage to purchase a cow, some chickens and even a pig once in a while. This was more to help reduce expenses than for any fun and/or relaxation. Each day before going to his job at Kernel's he would tend his animals and each evening he would do the same. The rest of the land, with the exception of a small backyard, was rented out to a local farmer and this money was used to offset the mortgage as well. Some of the crops were also shared and were used to feed the small number of animals that were kept for milk, butter, eggs and meat.

The remaining part of the plot of land near the buildings was used as a garden to grow vegetables. Joe's character and his attention to detail were shown in the tending of his garden as much as it was in his fabrication of glasses at his job as optician. Joe would carefully lay out rows with string, not by sight, but by meticulous measurements. The children would not be allowed to participate in the planting of the seedlings until Joe had carefully laid out the plots and prepared the soil. Once all the preparation was completed, then others could come and be a part of the process. Joe, in preparing his garden, was much like God preparing Joe for His service. Not until God had carefully prepared Joe was he going to be placed into the service of bringing others to God's kingdom. Just as the garden had to be weeded and pruned and carefully tended, Joe still had some weeds to be pulled from his life and old attitudes had to be pruned from his memories before his service could be utilized as God would have it.

The house was modest, with small rooms and stucco walls. When the Huffs moved into the home it was without a bathroom, but it did have running water which was a huge improvement to the house on State Road 421. It also had a furnace, which provided heat in the cold Indiana winters, but of course no air conditioning for the hot, humid summers, especially in late July and August. Instead of central air, the Huffs had three old, red, metal lawn chairs placed under the tallest and widest of the willow trees. There on the hottest days they would sit to stay as cool as possible. In contrast to the city where Joe could never get away from the heat, in the country he could sit beneath the tree and feel the unimpeded breeze blowing across his land. This escape from the heat of the city is another picture of Joe's escape from the clutches of his past.

Smoking was the final vice remaining from Joe's past and was soon to be gone. God had the final weeding to do. The tobacco was a hindrance to the harvest God had in store for Joe's life. This time it was with the help and accountability of Mary that caused Joe to finally kick his smoking habit. God used Mary and others to get tobacco out of Joe's life. Once again Joe's own words need to be used to explain how quickly an obstacle can be removed from a person's life if they are willing to let God lead.

And then on cigarettes. I had the very bad habit as usual, as a lot of people have. I was smoking three packs of king size a day. At noon I would smoke a cigar after lunch and at night I had a collection of pipes that I would go home and smoke. And like it (Bible) says, the Lord works in various ways. One night we were at Mary's folks and her mother says, "George, why don't you quit smoking?" And I said, "I'm going to." So that night on the way home I took out a cigarette, I'd just bought a carton that day, and I'd just opened a fresh pack and I'd only smoked about two out of it and I took another one and I stuck it in my mouth and I lit it. We were riding along and Mary said to me, "Why did you lie to my mother?" I said, "I didn't lie to your mother." She said, "Yes you did." I said, "Well what did I do?" She said, "You told her you were going to quit smoking." I said, "I just did." So the cigarette I had, I pinched it out the window; stuck it in my pocket. I went home and I laid the pack up, the cigarette on top of it, the carton was lying there. I walked past it day after day after day. I never touched it again. Before, if I would have tried I would have gotten irritable. Many times she told me that I should go ahead and smoke because I was worse than a bear with a sore nose. But this time I had help–the Lord. You see, like I say, he works in various ways. He didn't want me to drink. He didn't want me to smoke, because he had a plan, a plan that I should help others and not be detrimental to them. That I should be an example, not of drinking and smoking, but of doing without those things that I didn't need just to show His glory.

Just down the gravel road south of the new home of the Huff family was a structure that would become an integral part of God's plan for Joe's forgiveness on the way to His service. The structure was a small, white church called Fairview Christian. It was an unassuming structure, set out in the middle of a field and Joe and his family were firmly planted in the church. The congregation was easily fit into the little church and they couldn't afford a full-time pastor and had to rely on men who held other jobs through the week and would then serve the small flock on Sunday mornings.

It was after the move to Boone County and the move from Downing Avenue church to Fairview that Joe began to actively work in the church and God began to hoe, fertilize, and water Joe's Christian walk. God would soon harvest Joe and place him into service so he could help fulfill scriptures such as:

> "This is what the kingdom of God is like. A man scatters seed on the ground. Night and day, whether he sleeps or gets up, the seed sprouts and grows, though he does not know how. All by itself

the soil produces grain-first the stalk, then the head, then the full kernel in the head. As soon as the grain is ripe, he puts the sickle to it, because the harvest has come." Mark 4:26-29

Joe continued through this decade of his life to live and exemplify his steadfast dedication to his job, family and faith. Not only did he serve and protect his immediate family, but he also continued to open his home to members of Mary's family who had need of a place to live and even sometimes recuperate from injury. It would have been easy for Joe to turn them away, but again that was not in his character. He had seen the devastation his father, Guy, had lived through when he was injured and he couldn't bear the thought of anyone suffering like his father.

The height of his caring for family was probably when he welcomed Georgia and Arthur to live in a small trailer in the back of his home. Although he and Arthur had problems in the past and there were children born of Georgia and Arthur that could and should have welcomed them into their homes, the couple had a need for a place to live and Joe would not say no. He let them pull the trailer on to his farm and made them feel welcome in their new setting.

Even though other members of the extended family were important to Joe, the relationship between he and his three children was by far the most important. The memories his children have of the years of 1950 through 1960 are very fond to say the least. Unlike the memories of youth Joe had, he made absolutely sure the memories between he and his kids were pleasant and special. When asking his children about what they remember about these times, one quickly sees a smile and twinkle in their eyes as they reflect on the days spent with their dad.

From flying kites in the garden after the vegetables had been harvested to shooting baskets on the old rim nailed directly to the side of the old barn, Joe's kids speak lovingly and longingly about those most special times. Mentoring and loving his children and making sure they did not live through the experiences he lived through caused a chain of pain and heartache to be broken. Billy, Betty and Carol have such pleasant memories of their childhood they have in turn made sure to keep Joe's legacy alive and well in their children and their children's children.

While purposeful in his love and caring for the children, Joe's humor and mischievous nature would often come out. Joe would nurture and care for the kids; showing Billy how to milk and care for the animals, allowing Betty and Carol to help him in the garden. Then in the same evening Joe could be found playing jokes on his kids by showing up outside a window with his face pushed up against the glass. He laughed his most special laugh of glee in seeing his daughters scream at the sudden appearance of his nose plastered against the glass.

As the three siblings grew from young children into teenagers, their lives had the consistency, love and humor Joe's life had been void of all through his formative years. He was determined to and accomplished the difficult task of raising three wonderful children in a loving, caring and fun-filled life.

The things of Joe's past were never far from his thoughts and actions, but he chose those most positive actions and experiences of his past to share with his children. In those summer months Joe would often bring out his accordion or his harmonica and the family would sit out under the willow tree in the front yard and Joe would play and the family would sing Christian hymns. Joe's love of musical instruments and singing were pleasant, but these times shared with his family were a far cry from the days of Joe's youth of summer singing with the members of his gang on the way back from the parks of Indianapolis.

On these same summer evenings as the darkness began to overtake the front yard, the kids would gather around the red metal lawn chair on the cool grass and listen to Joe reminisce about his travel to foreign lands while he was in the Navy. Joe had a way of making the stories come to life and the lands seemed so real it was as if they had all been there and made them long to actually see these places he so vividly described. Had Joe been able to see inside his young teenaged son's head, he may not have made the Navy and the travels sound so pleasant.

Joe's dedication to his faith and work also continued to grow during this time. Joe was in his second decade with Kernel's and was still doing his job faithfully, taking his standard lunch, coming home, doing his chores while helping his son learn the ropes of farming and helping his daughters in their passage into adolescence. Also during this time all three children were growing in their walk with the Lord. By this stage in their lives Joe and Mary had the children firmly in the church.

Joe had successfully completed his mission of developing his family in a most positive and opposite way he had experienced. This is most noticeable in his son, Billy. Where Joe had no car as a youth, he made sure Billy had one. Where Joe had no boundaries, he made sure Billy had curfews, rules and accountability. Where Joe went to work and had to learn "on the job", he took the time to teach Billy how to work, then sent him out. Joe wanted to be sure his children's lives were the antithesis of his and he had accomplished this noble mission. Now it was time for God to use Joe in his work to help others in their faith.

The optical career that Joe had established provided an interesting parallel to the spiritual labors that would lie ahead for him. He was becoming more and more equipped with some of the tools of his faith and God would begin giving Joe opportunities to use them.

In the present day field of optometry, little attention is given to the making of eyeglasses. In fact, the need for glasses at all is being challenged with the advent of corrective laser eye surgery. It is common to see "One-hour" optical stores which is yet another testament to the highly technological and instant way of life. It's hard to imagine the picture of a man taking his bare hands, a piece of glass and a drum of sand and spending eight hours a day molding and shaping one eyeglass lens at a time. Yet

The Fifth Decade   107

this image was exactly the picture of nearly every day of Joe's work life at Kernel's in the late 1950s.

The art form known as Tribology, which describes the using of abrasives in shaping of things such as telescopes and eyeglasses has been chronicled all the way back to the annals of early mankind. As is known, glass is made of particles of sand. In much the same way as iron is used to shape itself when heated, sand can be used to grind glass to the proper perspective. Every day for most of his thirty-seven years of employment, Joe would stand over three large drums, each containing different coarseness of wet, colored sand and grind eyeglass lenses by hand. Not until the end of his career did machines start to take the place of the manual tasks required to do his job. In the center of each of the large, metal drums that were slightly rounded in the bottom, was a hard ball that rolled freely. Holding the lens in one hand, Joe would reach into the drum and take a handful of the wet sand then slowly bring it up and over the ball rubbing the sand over the glass, which was positioned on top of the ball. This methodical act of abrasion would eventually get the lens to the proper curvature and thickness for the required prescription.

Joe's job may have seemed tedious and mundane, but God used the time spent bent over the drums in the quiet solitude of the back room to reflect on and deepen his relationship with God. From this time of reflection, God instilled in Joe the desire to share his faith with others.

About this time, Joe began carpooling with a man into the city. The two became friends and during the course of the 45-minute trip one way back and forth to work, they began to deepen their relationship and delve into topics that lesser acquaintances may have deemed too personal. Over the course of time, the two men began talking more and more about things of a spiritual nature. This continued until one day, Joe ultimately shared the message of Jesus and His sacrifice for our sins and his friend made a commitment to accept Christ as his Lord and Savior. Joe's career was the perfect metaphor in describing how he touched the life of this friend. Joe was able to use the "coarseness" of his past to shape the spiritual lens of God's forgiveness in such a way that caused his friend to see his own life and need for God's grace more clearly.

Joe had turned the corner and was sprinting toward the finish of this section of his life, but just the beginning of his years of service. The decade of the sixties would begin with two more losses of loved ones; one permanent and one temporary. Joe's maturity in his faith however, would enable him to handle these losses in a much different manner than any he had experienced up to this point in his life.

SECTION THREE

Serving

"Serve wholeheartedly, as if you were serving the Lord, not men,…"
Ephesians 6:7

CHAPTER SIX

The Sixth Decade
1960-1970
Age 50-60

"You did not choose me, but I chose you and appointed you to go and bear fruit-fruit that will last. Then the Father will give you whatever you ask in my name."
John 15:16

The decade of age fifty to sixty began with the temporary loss of Joe and Mary's beloved son, Billy. Not in the spiritual sense, but the literal sense. Billy, in a parallel experience to his father, went into the service of his country by joining the Navy. The United States was at peace, but it was a tenuous peace at best. The Cold War was as intense as it could possibly be and the countries dedicated to communism, caused the Huff family to be very concerned about their son going off to serve in the military. There was also talk of involvement in Vietnam. Going back in the history of the family, Joe's parents were probably just as concerned when he went off to the service. After all when Joe went into his second stint into the Navy, WWII was on the horizon.

The difference between Billy and Joe was their ages. Joe was older in years and life experiences than was Billy. Billy had just graduated from high school and had been fortunate to have lived a much more sheltered life than had Joe. Even though experiences during the time in the Navy were probably very similar, the exit from the service and the support Billy had versus what Joe had was very different.

An example of this is Joe and Mary wanting to make sure when Billy returned home he would have a strong starting point so he would not have to struggle the way Joe and Mary had. The three-acre plot of land next to Joe and Mary came available for sale. They let Billy know and helped him purchase it. On a portion of the land there was an old house, although not a large, well kept or beautiful place, it was still livable and could be improved. So, during the four years away from home, Billy was beginning to build his life by sending money home from his monthly pay to invest in his future.

In 1961, Yuri Gagarin overcame the constraints of earth's gravity and launched a craft into outer space. Joe had lived through so many changes in his life to this point that it seemed unbelievable. In the early years of Joe's life, air travel was in its infancy and now it had gone to the point of leaving this earth and dreams of exploring other planets was soon to be a reality. With all these changes coming faster and faster, and everything going on in the world, there were times when no change would have been welcomed. This is not a reality of life's experiences and it was not a reality in Joe's life as well. Joe was about to experience another and permanent loss.

Georgia and Arthur were settling in to their life in rural Boone County in the small trailer near the back of Joe and Mary's house. Georgia had retired from the workforce when she and Arthur sold their home and purchased the small mobile home and moved. She had last worked at Ft. Benjamin Harrison and Arthur was retired as well. Their life was very simple and mundane, living in the small trailer with no air conditioning, and really no outside interests. It was not, however, without times of laughter and joy. In retrospect the memories of those watching the older couple brought smiles to those who shared this part of their life.

One such memory was the way Georgia would call Arthur when he had managed to sneak off to the barn to spend some time away from the small trailer and away from the direction and watchful eyes of Georgia. She would call first and when he wouldn't answer or didn't choose to answer, she would "trill" her tongue at a pitch that would send the local dogs running for cover. Arthur would then come sauntering back to see what he had done or should have done.

Georgia had long since been diagnosed with sugar diabetes and her health had been in a continually deteriorating pattern. Her disease had progressed to a stage where she was forced to give herself two shots a day to try and keep the illness at bay. For whatever reason, the disease, the marriage or simply the aging process, Georgia had become a very strong willed woman. She displayed many of the same characteristics of her only son. She was purposeful, direct and was definitely the leader of the two-person household.

She also showed the characteristic of being habitual in her actions. The disease forced her to be punctual when she medicated herself, but she also had the same meals, at the same time and at the same place on a daily basis. She didn't carry the metal lunch box with the leather strap handle that Joe did, but the sameness and routine of her life had been passed on to the son she loved so much.

The large, gray haired elderly lady could be found most days wearing in her very plain housedress sitting at the small table in the small trailer passing the hours playing solitaire. In the summer months when it got hot in the cramped, un-air conditioned quarters she would move to one of the red metal lawn chairs under the big willow tree.

Time, trauma and diabetes finally took their toll and Joe suffered the permanent loss mentioned earlier when Georgia passed away. Mary and the others in the Huff family had faithfully served Georgia by washing clothes, making meals and taking her to the doctor. Joe and his sister, Charlotte, lovingly cared for Georgia to the very end. Both Charlotte and Joe were at Georgia's bedside when she finally left this world behind. A woman who had lived through so much; two marriages, the loss of three children and a painful, debilitating disease, was comforted by the fact she was leaving behind a legacy of children who she was very proud of and loved dearly.

This permanent loss of Georgia did not make the temporary loss of Billy any easier. In fact, it caused Joe and Mary to worry even more about their absent son. The world was getting more and more dangerous and the news was filled with fact and speculation of the possibilities of all out war on at least two different fronts. The two areas were Cuba and the continuing escalation of the involvement in Vietnam. Joe and Mary's faith was continuing to grow, but after all this was their son and he was in harms way. Coupled with the loss of his mother, Joe just could not stand the thought of yet another tragedy in his life. Joe prayed fervently that his son would return safely from the Navy and asked that God would protect him. He desired affirmation that his prayers were being answered.

Billy was in a situation where he couldn't communicate often with his mother and father. Being on board ship and out to sea coupled with the uncertainties of the world situation made communication difficult to say the least. There would be times when several weeks might pass without word being received on the farm back in Boone County. During one of these times of void in communications, God took the opportunity to take Joe closer to the decision of service.

It was a late summer day in July and Joe was in the country house by himself. Being a warm and humid day, the windows had all been open to try and get as much fresh air into the stucco home as possible so that sleep might come easier that evening. This included the upstairs windows where the girls slept that were without screens. Joe had just listened to another of the doom and gloom newscasts of the troubling world situation.

In the solitude of his small, hot bedroom Joe went to his knees beside the bed and began to pray for his son's safety. He had never prayed with such fervor and precise requests. He wanted to know his son was safe and he wanted to be sure God had heard his prayers. As Joe recounted this experience, he specifically remembered that during this intense time of fellowship and communication with his Heavenly Father, he had to work at not being distracted by some noise that he kept hearing. He prayed specifically that God could give him some sort of validation that his prayers had reached His loving ears. He prayed for a "sign" from God.

As Joe completed his request and his intense time of fellowship with his Heavenly Father, he slowly opened his eyes and the first thing he saw was a small sparrow sitting quietly on the window ledge of the bedroom. The very first words that came to Joe's mind were the words of one of his favorite songs "His Eyes Are on The Sparrow." The stanza that came to his mind was:

"Let not your heart be troubled,
His tender word I hear,
And resting on His goodness,
I lose my doubts and fears;
Tho' by the path He leadeth
But one step I may see:
His eye is on the sparrow,
And I know He watches me;
His eye is on the sparrow,
And I know He watches me."

Author- Civilla Durfee Martin

The words of this song came to Joe's mind as he looked up and saw the sparrow calmly perched before him. Joe had sung this hymn many times in church as a young man on hiatus from his problems on those Sunday mornings of his youth. Never before had the words meant so much and it was if Joe had heard them himself for the very first time. He knew without a doubt that Billy was okay and would be coming home safely because God was watching out for him.

Joe would not have you believe that somehow the sparrow magically appeared in the room with no knowledge of how it got there. The fact that the upstairs windows were open that day gives reason to know how the bird got in, but the "why" is what God showed Joe in the words of the song.

Further proof that God was in control and orchestrating the events was revealed in what happened next. The sparrow is a small, spastic bird, yet as Joe walked toward the bird, it never moved. It simply looked at him as he approached and calmly allowed him to gather the small creature up in his gentle hands and walk to the door and on outside where he let the bird return to its own habitat. God had used the bird as a messenger to Joe that his prayers had been heard and answered.

During the years Billy was away and after the death of Georgia, another of the validations of Joe's kindness and caring was demonstrated by the fact he and Mary still continued to care for Arthur. Here was a situation where Arthur was really no blood relation to either Joe or Mary, but they still cared for him. Mary would wash his clothes and keep him as clean as she could and they would take him to town each week so he could buy his groceries and stop on the way home at the Dairy Bar for a chocolate shake. Arthur could have been looked upon as a burden to be shed, but he was treated as a family member to be cared for even when he became not very loveable in his later years. Again it was as if Joe was making sure the men in his life would not have to suffer.

God's promise to Joe through the appearance of the sparrow was fulfilled in the mid 1960's. Billy returned to Boone County and the small home he had purchased while away in the service. He came back to a job, home and quickly a family, which was much different than the way Joe had come back from his time in the Navy. Both Billy and Joe, however, had narrowly missed having to serve during all out war. Joe had gotten out just before the beginning of WWII and Billy got out just before the height of the Vietnam War. God had protected Billy much like he had Joe.

The instability of the times was in direct opposition to Joe's

The Sixth Decade

life during this period. JFK had been assassinated, Martin Luther King had given his "I have a dream" speech and the LA riots had taken place. The turmoil of the time seemed to threaten the very foundation of life in America. Not so in the Huff household. Everything seemed to be coming together for Joe and Mary and their lives were finally settled and normal. Billy, Betty and Carol were all married within a two-year period and what seemed like immediately, grandchildren began to appear on the scene. Joe's life was much like he hoped it could be. He was actively involved in his church and beginning to slow down and enjoy the fruits of his labor by traveling, bowling and being a part of his grandchildren's lives. All this gave Joe a picture of life that most could only dream of, certainly beyond any of his dreams.

Joe's journey through life had taken him to the sixth stage of Shakespeare's Seven Ages of Man and he was content in his "lean and slippered pantaloon, with spectacles on nose and pouch on side." Joe was content with where his life was, but his Heavenly Father wasn't. God had other plans for Joe. To stay where he was and in his comfort zone was not in God's plan for Joe's life and the lives he would touch.

As Joe crossed the halfway point of his sixth decade, he was at the edge of another compelling transition in his life. It's a time most look forward to with mixed emotions. The fruits of labor come into being, yet the realization that all die a physical death some day begins to enter into the mindset with more regularity. What is life really all about anyway? For those who don't have the assurance of spending eternity in heaven this can be a source of much worry and fear. Thankfully, God offers a way for each person to be rid of this fear and rest in the hope of spending forever with Him in a place wonderful beyond description. This peace of mind and heart that exceeds all human understanding was a gift Joe was about to receive.

He was well established in his career now and while not a glamorous vocation, the stability had provided him the opportunity to place his energies on other things he valued more, namely his role as husband and father. Joe had never gone the route so many do, the course of chasing after the esteem and allure of professional or social fame. He purposefully chose to remain in the shadows where things were known and consistent. Life had given him enough hair-raising experiences; he didn't want to pay the price that could come as a result of pursuing the materialism of the "American Dream." Instead, Joe had decided a couple of decades earlier that his legacy would be centered in his family and a select few others who were associated with him and he had performed admirably thus far in the building of his legacy.

Joe was deriving much joy from his life across nearly all facets. There was much to be content about with his career humming along and the satisfaction of seeing his children leave the nest into adulthood and beginning to establish their own families and lives. After overcoming so much in his past and enduring to this point, Joe felt like he was complete in every way imaginable, or at least in every way that was important to him. On top of the satisfaction that his fatherly role was bringing, his marriage was stronger than ever. And, unlike his twenties and thirties when trouble seemed to reach out and grab him, Joe now felt firmly in control of his destiny—things were good.

All strive for contentment and control in their lives and Joe was no different. People achieve it in many different ways and at different times, or more appropriately, they *perceive* that it is being attained. The challenge with this control issue, however, is that all reach a point where it is necessary to wrestle with the issue of God's plans instead of their own. Joe had no reason to assume God had any unresolved issues with him. He was very active in his church serving as the Sunday School Superintendent and also as a Deacon. He had fulfilled his responsibility of making sure his children were raised under the influences of the church, and he had rid himself completely of the moral vices that plagued him for so many years. What Joe didn't understand, like so many others, is that he had never fully reconciled the sins of his past with God. Outwardly he had put aside his old ways, but inwardly he was leading his life based on his own wishes, not according to the will of the Heavenly Father. While he was performing the works of one who believes in God, his heart and soul had not been surrendered completely. It was this aspect of control that God had issue with and it was time for that to be revealed to Joe in a dramatic and life-changing way.

This hidden struggle with God over control of his life reached a climactic point with Joe in the spring of 1966 and he was completely blind-sided. Not the physical blindness that the Apostle Paul suffered in biblical times, but with similar ramifications. In the prime of his boxing career, Joe had vowed to himself that he would use his toughness and speed to never get knocked to his knees by an opponent. He was in a different kind of struggle now and it wasn't with a foe, but instead with his Heavenly Father who loved him more than he ever realized. It is a love so strong that despite sinfulness, God provides a way to be made righteous in His sight. There is nothing one can do to earn His favor; one only needs to give his or her heart over to Him. On a very special night at the age of fifty-six, God brought Joe to his knees in total submission, and with a flood of emotion brought all his past transgressions to bear. Yet at the same time, by laying his sins before the throne of heaven, Joe experienced in a glorious way the matchless and unfailing love of God that He pours out on those who belong to Him.

> *But as the Bible says, often times we backslide and I had backslid plenty, but now I was coming back and back and back to the Lord. I worked in the church. I'd worked as a Sunday school teacher. I'd worked as the Superintendent and also was a Deacon in the church. I thought my life was complete until one night like Paul on the road to Damascus that sweet little man, that kind, loving, kind to everyone, he loved all people, he did something that I said a man would never do. Like Paul, he put me on my knees and like Paul I said, "Lord, what will you have me to do?" I*

rededicated my life to Him. Then things became brighter. There was more understanding. There was so much love.

At the time of Saul's (later renamed Paul) encounter, he was persecuting those who followed Christ more aggressively than he ever had before. Joe did not share this characteristic with Paul, yet they did share the same predicament. Neither realized their need for submitting to God nor did they realize what God had in store for them once they surrendered the control of their lives.

"As he neared Damascus on his journey, suddenly a light from heaven flashed around him. He fell to the ground and heard a voice say to him, "Saul, Saul why do you persecute me?" "Who are you, Lord?" Saul asked. "I am Jesus, whom you are persecuting," he replied. "Now get up and go into the city, and you will be told what you must do.""Acts 9:3-6

Now that Joe was firmly committed to God he, like Paul, would endure a short time of waiting and reflecting on the magnitude of what had just happened. The idea that Joe could have turned his back on God for so many years and still be restored and welcomed into His loving arms was beyond comprehension. In the human way of thinking, it is difficult to grasp the things of God and one of those concepts is that in order to be in right fellowship with Him, control of one's life must be given over completely. It's a perfect contradiction that was perfectly conceived by an all-knowing Creator. Fully committing to Christ is very challenging. There are few things that will prove more difficult to master. It also goes against everything the world would prescribe, a world that calls for looking out for the individual first. It could have seemed even more illogical for someone like Joe who was entering the twilight years of his life. A time all look forward to when hopefully things can be enjoyed that have been worked for over so many years. However, despite

The Sixth Decade

being in his mid fifties and having navigated through all the challenges that had been brought his way, Joe now found himself in uncharted waters once again, not knowing which way to go or what to do next.

This encounter with God took Joe back to the beginning, and he was experiencing a spiritual rebirth. All of a sudden he found himself completely dependent on a Higher Power. These waters were distinctly different, though, than the waters he had crossed in his life so far. No longer was he being tossed in the frothy waves of a stormy sea. Now the waters were tranquil, warm and inviting. There was a strange, but glorious peace in his heart giving him a welcomed confirmation that he was in the right place. It was the perfect contrast to where he had been nearly forty years earlier. During his duty in the Navy while searching for direction in his life, he was taken off course because he lacked the one thing that was now revealed to him. He was trying to be his own navigator for all those many years, but now he was willing to release control of the compass and maps and let God tell him where to go. Paul talked about this in his message to the church at Ephesus as he encouraged them to be unified in their faith.

> *"Then we will no longer be infants, tossed back and forth by the waves, and blown here and there by every wind of teaching and by the cunning and craftiness of men in their deceitful scheming. Instead, speaking the truth in love, we will in all things grow up into him who is the Head, that is, Christ."*
> *Ephesians 4:14-15*

After accepting Jesus as Lord and Savior, the Bible calls for striving towards a level of maturity in one's faith. That maturity comes in large part from simply being obedient to God and serving Him where He is and by doing the things He directs. It is a process of emptying the heart of selfish ambition so there is more room for God to come and dwell and guide through the

Holy Spirit who is promised to any person upon acceptance of Jesus. Out of obedience, Joe began an earnest search for God's plan for the rest of his life. He could never have imagined what God had in store.

> *Then I started praying, "Lord, tell me what you want me to do." So one night he answered me. He said, "I want you to preach." I was 56 years old. And like Moses I said, "Lord, you don't know what you're asking me. I can't do it." He said, "You can." I said, "Well Lord I can't even get up in front of the congregation and sing. Every time I do I break out in a sweat. Even the people make fun of me and say that I should carry a bath towel with me." He said, "I'll take care of that." I said, "But Lord, how am I going to preach? I don't know enough about preaching." It was then that he laid a verse of scripture on my heart. The verse says in Romans 12:2*
>
> *"Do not conform any longer to the pattern of this world, but be transformed by the renewing of your mind. Then you will be able to test and approve what God's will is–his good, pleasing and perfect will."*
>
> *And I said, "Lord what can I do? I don't know enough to go through all that." And He said, "You can go to school." I said, "Lord at my age you want me to go to school?" I said, "I have no idea. I have a family. Where am I going to school? I can't leave and go to another state and go to school." He said, "I'll take care of it." He said, "Turn to the Yellow Pages." I did. And then it seemed to pop out at me just like it had come out of the paper. There was the name of the college. He said, "Call." I did and I heard a voice on the telephone. A voice that, as long as I live, I'll never forget. A man speaking he said, "Can I help you?" A man that I learned to love, to respect; it was one of the teachers. I had him in class for four years that I went to school. And I graduated four years later in 1969. Then I was 60 years old.*

So there it was. God had given Joe an answer to his question. The last time he had been in an educational setting was thirty plus years ago at Optician school in Michigan. Now he was faced with the challenge of going back to school, this time Seminary, to be of all things a preacher. The man who had spent his entire adult life working comfortably in the shadows of a back room was being asked to step out into the light and behind the pulpit to share God's message with others.

Joe's calling to the ministry was a great example of how God can use people regardless of their perceived abilities or how others may view them. The gospel of John, Chapter 15 talks about the Vine and the Branches. The essence of the story is the idea that God is the main source of everything a person should be about as a follower of Him and apart from Him one can do nothing. He is the Vine and His people are merely the Branches or the recipients of His nourishment and strength. In fact, a main reason for people being here on this earth is merely to glorify God. While all the other things of life are important and valuable, existing without God at the center of one's life is a futile exercise in frustration. Yet once aligned with Him, everything begins to make sense or at the very least, seem possible. Such was the case with Joe. When so many others could have looked at him and scoffed at the idea of going back to school at this stage in his life, to Joe there was no alternative. He had received his direction and he knew he had to follow it.

In 1967, just a year into Joe's journey through seminary, the field of medicine enjoyed one of its most celebrated achievements with the first successful heart transplant. Joe's heart was experiencing something magical at that time as well. While not being transplanted, it was definitely being transformed as he devoted himself to the task of learning the finer details of his deepening, personal relationship with Jesus. To those who were close to him, the transformation in Joe's life was both sudden and drastic. It's not that he was leading a sinful life just before his Paul-like encounter; he wasn't. But during this time Joe developed a passion and focus for God unlike anything else he had ever done.

Making eyeglasses, boxing, singing and playing music, nothing compared to the priority he was now giving his studies. Joe seemed to always have his books out at home when anyone would visit, and he was quick to share what he was learning with whomever was around. His conversation topics changed from all the other things that he used to identify with to issues that dealt with his new identity in Christ.

He was still working full-time and taking classes at night. Even the regimented routine of his daily lunch was not important any longer, as Joe utilized the time to prepare for class. Joe was fully immersing himself in the things of God as he followed in the footsteps of Paul, his unseen spiritual mentor, who modeled so wonderfully what it means to shift one's priorities away from everything except God. In another one of Paul's letters he related what this priority shift is supposed to be like for all who call themselves Christians.

> *"But whatever was to my profit I now consider loss for the sake of Christ. What is more, I consider everything a loss compared to the surpassing greatness of knowing Christ Jesus my Lord, for whose sake I have lost all things. I consider them rubbish, that I may gain Christ and be found in him, not having a righteousness of my own that comes from the law, but that which is through faith in Christ–the righteousness that comes from God and is by faith." Philippians 3:7-9*

God's grace is truly unfathomable. Just like everything else He inspires, it is perfect and complete in every way. When someone trusts God to forgive sins, they are wiped clean as if taking a polishing cloth to a tarnished piece of silver. He makes people pure again in His sight and restores them back into fellowship with Him just as an earthly father would do to a child returning from a wayward rebellion.

God provided glorious symbolism to Joe each night that he made his way to class. The seminary God had directed him to was located back in the heart of the very same city where so many of his earlier transgressions had occurred. What a better way to reveal to Joe that the sins of his past had been totally and completely forgiven. The site of countless battles with evil was now the place of Joe's eternal victory by the grace of God. Imagine what someone who knew Joe from his time in the city before would have thought seeing him march up the steps and through the doors of the seminary carrying his silver, metal lunchbox in one hand and his Bible and school books in the other. That couldn't be the same Joe who was known around town for his carousing and acts of revelry? The one who was in the gang, barely got through high school and didn't ever seem to have a steady job? Surely he must not know he is going into the wrong building?

Nothing is beyond the capabilities of a sovereign God who can see all the good in each person of His creation and with one stroke, brush away all the bad and empower people to do things in His service that were not thought possible. This account of Paul taken just a few days after his conversion on the road to Damascus after being relieved of his temporary blindness is an example of what God can do to even the most unsuspecting person. Joe must have seen himself in the very same context

"Saul spent several days with the disciples in Damascus. At once he began to preach in the synagogues that Jesus is the Son of God. All those who heard him were astonished and asked, "Isn't he the man who raised havoc in Jerusalem among those who call on this name? And hasn't he come here to take them as prisoners to the chief priests?" Yet Saul grew more and more powerful and baffled the Jews living in Damascus by proving that Jesus is the Christ." Acts 9:19b-22

Joe performed magnificently throughout his years in seminary, earning an "A" in nearly every course. He also was quick to share the credit for his achievement with others. Mary had supported, exhorted and affirmed Joe all through his years of study in preparation for service. The gift God had given to Joe in the form of his wife Mary was one Joe did not take lightly. Mary also knew and was thankful for Joe being a part of her life and the father for their children that she had prayed for through the early years of their marriage.

When Joe graduated from school, Mary wanted to give him the best gift she could possibly give. As soon as Joe had started school, Mary dreamed of being able to give him a trip he would never forget. Not to some exotic, tropical island or any of the traditional vacation spots, but to the Holy Land. Besides her love and support, this one gift could finalize and affirm all Joe had been studying.

The trip was more than Joe or Mary could ever have imagined. For four years Joe had been studying the history of the Bible and reading and studying God's Word and now he, with Mary at his side, had been able to actually walk in the very same footsteps where Jesus had walked. This made all the events and visual images Joe had in his mind come to life in a way he would never forget. Many times through the rest of his life Joe would be heard telling stories of his memories of this most eventful trip.

God had used many people to prepare Joe for his life of service. In this latest chapter of Joe's life God had used the men in his school, his children, other loved ones and most especially Mary to finalize his path to service. The protection had been perfect, the forgiveness complete and it was time for Joe to follow God's direction into his life of service to his Lord and Savior.

CHAPTER SEVEN

The Seventh Decade
1970-1980
Age 60-70

"Therefore I glory in Christ Jesus in my service to God."
Romans 15:17

Near the end of Jesus ministry on this earth, after His arrest and before His crucifixion, the Roman soldiers shoved a crown of thorns down onto Jesus' head to mock His claim of being the Messiah sent from God. Jesus was coming to the end of time of service in man form and in the Word one can sense urgency in His actions and deeds to be sure the Father's work was completed. Joe, to use another analogy, was nearing the end of his journey through the "Seven Ages of Man." Looking back at this decade of his life, one can sense urgency in Joe's life of service as well. The seventh decade of his life was to be one full of service. Having only the short time of his life left, Joe felt a deep desire to spend a concentrated, consecrated life of devotion to the God who had protected, forgiven and prepared him for the service he was about to undertake.

On the trip to the Holy Land after graduation from seminary, Joe had purchased a replica of the crown of thorns. It was brought back from the land of Jesus and lovingly placed on a cross in front of the pulpit at Fairview Christian Church. For Joe, this replica signified the beginning of his ministry on this earth. Joe knew that at his advanced age he had but a few years to preach the gospel and one could sense the urgency he felt to be sure as many as possible could be given the truth of God's plan of salvation through acceptance of Jesus Christ as Lord and Savior.

Joe's four years of seminary training could be compared to the sport he loved so much, boxing. Just as the boxer preparing for a fight to the finish, Joe had spent a lifetime of experience and preparation to join God's corner of the battle for souls. The last four years of Joe's life had been intense work just like the intense workouts a boxer has to have immediately before a fight. Joe had been in the ring of battle for lost souls for all his life. The big difference now was he was in the opposite corner. For years Joe had been in Satan's corner, now he was embarking on the battle against Satan and God had used all of Joe's life experience as his training regiment to prepare for the good fight, not with man, but with the evil one for the souls of man.

The boxer has little protection from his opponent when he enters the ring, but Joe had been prepared well and was now armed with knowledge through his schoolwork and God's direction in what he should do. Joe now went into the ring to battle Satan with the "full armor of God" in place.

"Finally, be strong in the Lord and in his mighty power. Put on the full armor of God so that you can take your stand against the devil's schemes. For our struggle is not against flesh and blood, but against the rulers, against the authorities, against the powers of this dark world and against the spiritual forces of evil in the heavenly realms. Therefore put on the full armor of God, so that when the day of evil comes, you may be able to stand your ground, and after you have done everything, to stand. Stand firm then, with the belt of truth buckled around your waist, with the breastplate of righteousness in place, and with your feet fitted with the readiness that comes from the gospel of peace. In addition to all this, take up the shield of faith, with which you can extinguish all the flaming arrows of the evil one. Take the helmet of salvation and the sword of the Spirit, which is the word of God." Ephesians 6:1-17

Joe was now like a boxer in his prime or a warrior ready for battle. He couldn't have been prepared in any better manner and he was at the top of his game. Now, he just had to execute everything he had been trained to do. Just like athletes, this is not always easy, but Joe was up for the challenge. He began this climb into the ring of ministry much like he did everything else. Not in a loud, flamboyant entrance but in a quiet, unassuming walk seemingly unnoticed. An example of this quiet march to the ring could be seen manifested in the change in his lunch pail. For thirty plus years Joe had taken the same sandwich, cookies, orange and cold coffee in his old, silver, beat up lunch pail. Now, however, there was an addition to the usual culinary delight; now there was a package of tracts bound by a single rubber band on top of the beloved lunch. Now, the food for the soul was more important than the food for the body. At every opportunity Joe would share his new addition to his lunch with others with whom he came in contact. Joe had not officially climbed into the ring of serving a church full-time, but he had already started warming up by punching at Satan through other, more personal ways of service.

In all phases of Joe's life this sense of urgency seemed to kick in. Joe's actions, as well as his words, show that he realized how much of his short time on earth had been in Satan's corner and to live his life and influence all he could, Joe took every opportunity afforded him. This is not to say his life with his family and friends was forgotten, it just came in second to his opportunity to serve God. He still was the playful, funny, jokester he had always been, but everyone could tell his life had new meaning now that he was in God's corner.

Joe's passion to live life to its fullest could also be seen in his desire to travel and see God's creation. This rebirth and redirection in Joe's life was being manifested through the new eyes and heart God had given him. Joe was now seeing his world in a new light. One such trip was taken with one of his daughters, her husband and their three children. Joe, Mary and the others went to California to visit one of Joe and Mary's friends from the early days on Rawls Avenue in Indianapolis.

On the way west, Joe was adamant that he wanted to see the Grand Canyon. Even though some of the other family members didn't want to go "out of their way" to see the magnificent attraction, Joe insisted. He had always dreamed of standing on the precipice of the rim and looking over at the awesome creation of God. Since making his commitment to serve, this desire had even become stronger. Those who were blessed to be there on the day it finally happened would never forget what they experienced. As Joe climbed from the red station wagon where all had been crammed in for hours and slowly walked to the edge of the canyon, it was much like what was described above as a boxer slowly walking to the ring. Once Joe got to the edge, he stopped and looked across the great span and tears began to flow down his cheeks. These were tears of joy and thankfulness that God had brought him to this place. He was on the edge of the canyon wall, he was on the edge of his life of dedicated service and God had brought him to both places at the same time. At the time of this event, those who witnessed it probably didn't understand why this grown man was crying while staring out over the Grand Canyon, but now they understand and feel honored to have been a part of the event.

Joe was still warming up for the big event, his full time ministry position, and had many opportunities to continue his training. There was never a time Joe didn't answer the bell to serve. To complete his training and be ready to serve God the way it was intended, Joe retired from his full-time position at Kernel's Optical. After thirty-seven years of going daily to the quiet solitude of his small area in downtown Indianapolis, Joe was now able to serve others on a daily basis. He wasted no time. He immediately signed on as a volunteer at the hospital in the town near their home. Joe used this opportunity to serve the patients by taking them to and from therapy, but also used the time to visit and minister to those who had spiritual needs as well as physical needs. He quickly became a fixture in the hospital and was there any time they would have him.

During these times of service, Joe would still show his mischievous nature and good-hearted teasing and would do so at every opportunity with nurses and other volunteers, getting them to laugh on a regular basis. In the midst of pain and suffering, Joe would lighten the atmosphere. The people, patients and family members appreciated this pause in the trauma of illness that was severe enough to cause a hospital stay. On many occasions Joe would wear the remnants of lipstick on the top of his now balding head where some appreciative nurse, patient or family member had planted a "thank you" kiss.

Joe also was able to spend time bringing the Gospel message to the residents of the local nursing home. On Sunday mornings before God placed him in a church pulpit, Joe would leave his service at Fairview Christian Church and go directly to the nursing home and bring the message of salvation to those who could not get out to attend their own church. Only God knows how many souls were saved through this effort.

In typical "Joe" fashion, there was also laughter in this service. Joe, not even thinking about what he was saying, would announce to any family gathered at the house that he was going to conduct services at the nursing home for the "old folks." When looking at Joe's age at this time, sixty-five to seventy, he was older than many he was preaching to, but he still referred to them in that way. The further irony of his work at this facility would come later in Joe's life, but without laughter, when he would end up in a struggle over his own health.

During this time of service to God, Joe and Mary had many blessings. God had provided for them in a very real way. Coming from nothing at the beginning of their marriage, they now had not only a home in the country, but they were also able to eventually build their dream home on the lot next to the old house on Fairview Road. It had taken much sacrifice and effort on both Joe and Mary's part, but now as the time of service had gone into warp speed, God continued to heap on the blessings by providing this new home.

The home was not a mansion or overdone in any way, it was a simple three bedroom, one and a half bath brick ranch home with a full, unfinished basement. It was built just north of the existing house where they could watch as every board was nailed and every brick was laid. The old house had many memories for the Huff family and those memories could remain fresh because the old home could be seen from the new. The new house was to be full of memories as well, especially for all the grandchildren who were now being added on seemingly a yearly basis. The outside of the house was red brick with white trim, a one and one-half car garage with a horseshoe drive in front. The front yard was large and, of course, treeless. Treeless until Joe's loving hands began to plant trees and bushes along the road and down the side of the lot. The yard was a perfect place for all the young grandchildren to come and play.

In addition to the three bedrooms and one and a half baths of Joe and Mary's modest, brick home there was an informal family room. It had a fireplace at one end with a mantle running the full width of the wall. The mantle, covering the entire span of the concrete shelf, contained pictures of all their family members. The pictures served as a visual reminder of the legacy that Joe was so proud to be leaving the world. A sliding glass door looked out over the backyard, which was marked by a white board fence. Beyond the fence was more property that was usually overgrown with higher vegetation and contained a small pond. There was a small, dilapidated house located about an acre behind the fence that provided the grandchildren with the material for many a thrilling mystery story. The house had actually been used by some of the family about ten years or so past. A couch was located along the wall opposite the sliding glass door and next to the door sat Joe's leather recliner, which faced the fireplace wall and a little television that was off in the corner.

The scene of Joe sitting in his recliner watching television was not very common. He was not one, especially at this time in his life, to spend what to him was a golden opportunity for rich experiences, passively in front of the television. In fact, most of the time when family was visiting Joe would be up and participating in some activity, usually with the grandchildren. He was a wonderfully playful grandfather. He loved to tease the kids sometimes by corralling them between his arms and legs as he sat down. He would invariably keep one of the children in his little trap until they yelled for Grandma to come to the rescue much to the delight of the ornery Joe who reveled in the opportunity to cause a little mischief. It was the kind of game kids love to play because it had just the right mixture of glee and terror. How close could you get to Grandpa before you were snatched up in his large, muscular arms to be held captive until you pleaded for mercy? And of course, the kids loved to see Grandpa get "chastised" by his loving wife when the screams for help got to a level no one could ignore.

The one exception to not watching TV when family was over was when there happened to be a boxing match. One of the most memorable images for those who loved Joe was watching him watch a fight on TV. Despite his age, one would have thought he was ready to step into the ring at a moment's notice. As the two boxers squared off against one another employing the various tactics known to the sport, Joe would be moving his head, shoulders and arms as if he was right in the midst of the battle. As the boxers ducked, he would duck. As punches were thrown, he would shift in his chair and motion as if delivering his own counterpunch. It was much more entertaining for those in the room to watch him than it was to pay attention to what was being broadcast onto the glass screen in the corner. He still had a love and a passion for the sport and for athletics in general and it was obvious to everyone that they were in the presence of someone reliving shining moments of the past when he was at his physical prime. To see the intensity on his face and the swiftness of his movements, everyone knew he must have been a fierce opponent for whoever chose to climb into the ring with him.

One year for Joe's birthday he received the ultimate gift—a set of boxing gloves. Unfortunately for some of the grandchildren, this meant being led down into the unfinished basement of the home for a little "sparring session" with Grandpa. This ritual was repeated on nearly every visit and it almost invariably led to the same result. After a few minutes of fun-loving play, Joe would tap one of the kids on the nose just firm enough for them to realize they were up against a much superior opponent. As the child raced up the stairs near tears with a shiny red nose, Joe would dutifully follow knowing that he was about to receive another loving chastisement. Sure enough, as he emerged through the door at the top of the stairs, there would be his wee opponent in the arms of Grandma waiting for Grandpa to get his discipline. The small, mischievous smile on his face as he stood in the little hallway was a precious memory that has been seared in the minds of his family as if it was yesterday. He never hurt any of his grandchildren, nor would he ever have even thought of such a thing, but his competitiveness combined with that wonderful ornery streak couldn't be held back when the gloves were on. Everyone who had the privilege of knowing Joe is so thankful that God made him that way.

Joe's refusal to waste any opportunity for sport or play and his drive to take it on with urgency and intensity was the same way he approached his spiritual life in this all-important time of service. Looking back on the way he lived this decade it is obvious that Joe sensed the importance of maximizing every opportunity he had to share his faith with others. Much like the scrappiness he demonstrated as a boxer, he was now attacking the enemy with the same ferocity and energy as a fighter down on points and clawing to snatch victory from the clutches of defeat. Joe now had the peace in his heart that eternal victory had already been won for him on the cross, but he was determined to bring as many others along with him as he could, and he knew there wasn't much time to accomplish the mission he had been given.

After serving as interim pastor for a period of time, God was now ready for Joe to take on a full-time assignment. Two churches approached him at the same time and asked him to come and be their pastor. As a sign of maturity in his relationship with God, Joe would not commit to either one until he was sure he knew which one God had in mind.

> *I was a full-time minister as a part-time filling in and so forth. This went on for a while and finally two churches came and asked me if I would come and fill the pulpit. I said, "I can't make a commitment, I will come and preach." I said, "I'll preach at both of them and you can make up your mind as to whether you want me or not." Well, I went to the first one and I preached. They came to me and they said, "We'll take you." And I said, "I'm sorry, I haven't been to the other one yet." So I went to the other church and I preached and they said, "We'll take you." Well, here I had two churches. I said, "Lord what am I supposed to do?" He said, "Pray." And I prayed and I prayed and I prayed. Finally he laid on my heart just the one that I should take.*

The one he was supposed to take turned out to be a small, country church about an hours drive one-way from his home. It was a church that had been without effective leadership for some time. The situation had reached a critical point and the remaining congregation needed someone to step in or the church was doomed to become extinct. To Joe, the task was simple. He was just supposed to be there, that's all that really mattered. Unlike what many would have been tempted to do, he didn't spend a lot of time initially trying to set up an elaborate plan of restoring the church to some desired level of prominence. Instead, his thoughts and efforts were devoted exclusively to the spiritual condition of the hearts of the people he was there to serve. This was one of the benefits of the fact that God had called him into service later in his life. He didn't have a personal agenda. He had no desire to develop a name for himself or achieve any degree of notoriety. He was there to serve and to win souls for Christ, nothing more and nothing less.

To prepare his sermons, Joe used another part of the home. This special place, that meant so much to the family and most especially to Joe, was his study. It was located in the middle of the rectangular-shaped, one-story structure with a window facing the front yard where he could see his beloved red maple trees that he had planted and nurtured shortly after the house had been built. The front yard sloped gradually away from the house and past a flagpole, where Joe faithfully raised and lowered Old Glory on a daily basis. The slope continued until it reached the rural country road that served as the address for the now Reverend George and Mary Huff.

Inside the small, dimly lit eight by ten foot study were just a few pieces of wooden furniture that went along with the hardwood floor. There was a rocking chair that sat in one corner and was almost always used more for holding items important to Joe at the time than it was for rocking. Along the back wall beneath the window was a baby crib made of dark colored wood. For someone who didn't know Joe very well, it would have seemed entirely out of place in what otherwise was a very masculine domain. But this item carried with it a tremendous amount of significance to Joe. The crib dated back to the early nineteenth century and had served as the bedtime resting place for generations of Joe's family members. At least six generations had slept in that little cradle over the years, but while it was in his study, it served as a reminder for him of his childhood and his siblings, including his little sister Edna.

The third and most important piece of furniture in this spiritual sanctuary was a wooden roll-top desk that faced the front wall, just to the right upon entering the room. This was the spot where Joe spent countless hours having quiet time alone with God, studying his Bible and preparing his sermons. Pulled up to the desk was a heavy, metal rolling chair with padded cushions. Three wooden bookcases lined the right-side wall of the study and contained all the books and items that Joe had accumulated and deemed worthy of keeping over his lifetime, most of them reflecting his dedication to God. He had kept all the books that were used in his coursework at seminary. He had two family Bibles that had been passed down from his parents. He also had articles from his Holy Land trip that he kept in a lower section covered by doors in the middle bookshelf. There were things from his years of working as an optician and an assortment of obscure knick-knacks that had appealed to his playful side at some point or another.

Joe's office was extremely important to him and he treated it as a place of worship. No one was allowed inside without being accompanied by Joe himself. When he took people there, he would introduce his visitors to each item with the same reverence as an art gallery tour guide demonstrating a priceless Picasso. The experience of getting the "tour" of the office was very exciting for the grandchildren. It was his way of showing the legacy he was leaving for the family, a way of saying, "This is who I am—the place where I do the thinking and studying and preparing that will hopefully make a difference in someone's life."

The office also served as a wonderful closure to a struggle that Joe had undergone for sixty years. It was his final set of boundaries. Ultimately, God had provided for him everything he needed and it could all be found in that small, quiet space that was his study. It was the place where he talked to His Father, the ultimate role model he now had found. Someone he could fellowship with day and night, twenty-four hours a day. Someone who always had an answer and who Joe knew loved him and wanted only the best for him. This same, special relationship is there for any who call on His name. It was this relationship, and the overwhelming peace and joy that accompany it, that served as the motivation for the message he knew had to be told to those God placed in his path.

Joe prepared for his sermons on Sunday in a very simple, straightforward manner. He would sit at his small, roll-top desk with his Bible and some paper to write on. He used some of the reference materials that he had accumulated, but there was no vast theological library to pull from. He couldn't use a high-speed connection and hop on the Internet, in fact; he didn't even use a computer. Instead, he used a small Webster XL500 manual typewriter to put his notes into final form to take to the pulpit. It was light blue in color and was stored in a darker blue vinyl case with a zipper. The typewriter could be used while still inside the case by unzipping the cover and folding it back, but Joe preferred to remove it each time. Because it was manual, it was heavy for its size weighing eleven pounds. It was approximately one foot wide by one foot deep and three and a half inches tall. The four rows of keys were elevated each row a little higher than the one below like seats in a stadium. The tops of the keys were made of hard plastic that had a pearl-like color with black lettering. The top of the machine had the typical features of a manual typewriter. There was the roller that the paper wrapped around which also served as the hard surface that the metal bar would strike against as each letter was imprinted on the paper. It also had the metal lever protruding from the right side that was pushed from right to left when it was time to return the carriage to start a new line of words. Finally, there was the small metal guide that was pressed down onto the paper holding it against the roller and also serving as a reference for page margins. Joe's metal guide was covered with a fair amount of dried, white correction fluid that had collected over the years of use when painting over a letter that had been mistakenly pressed. To add to the laborious nature of preparing his sermons was the fact that Joe didn't know how to type. He used his two index fingers in a slow, methodical pecking, which worked just fine for the cause. For Joe, it was much more about quality anyway.

Just like the process that was used to prepare them, Joe's ser-

The Seventh Decade

mons were very simple and focused on a consistent theme. He didn't spend much time on Sundays dealing with topical issues of the day. He wasn't one to preach on controversial subjects nor did he tell many stories or try to make his sermons appeal to a broad set of interests. Instead he chose to focus on the souls who placed themselves in the pews, their spiritual needs and where each would spend eternity. The message was all about Christ. What he had done for Joe and what he offered anyone and everyone else who would accept the grace that is available to all. It was very important to Joe not to stray very far from the simple message of salvation that is presented in the Bible. He didn't soften the warnings the Bible contains nor did he sensationalize the promises. He spoke about Heaven and Hell and what each meant. He did his best to merely relay the words God inspired to those who penned them.

> *"Each one should use whatever gift he has received to serve others, faithfully administering God's grace in its various forms. If anyone speaks, he should do it as one speaking the very words of God. If anyone serves, he should do it with the strength God provides, so that in all things God may be praised through Jesus Christ. To him be the glory and power forever and ever. Amen."*
> *I Peter 4:10-11*

Freedom Christian Church, the place of Joe's full-time pastorate, was a typical Midwestern country church. It was extremely simple in its construction. The outside was made of wooden shingles painted white. In front of the church was a small, gravel parking lot capable of holding only a handful of cars. To the right of the church was a message board with a bell on top. Joe would ring the bell each Sunday by pulling on a long rope signaling the coming start of the service.

Entering the building required going up no more than a half dozen steps and once inside, the sanctuary was immediately there. The main floor contained no other interior walls and was slightly above ground level to accommodate the small, unfinished basement below which was used for Sunday school. The basement was accessed by a discreet set of stairs located off to the left upon entering the church. There was no foyer, welcome center or even classrooms. When walking through the double front doors, one would see two rows of pews down either side. The walkway led right from the front door straight to the pulpit in the front of the church, which was elevated slightly on a small platform.

It was the perfect setting for a purposeful, straightforward and personal minister like Joe. There was no choice of sneaking up into a balcony on a Sunday morning or secretly sliding into a chair in the back of the church. If entering the service late, attendees would be looking right at Joe standing in the pulpit, and they were guaranteed that he would be looking right back at them. Everyone coming to Joe's church was sure to be noticed and once inside, was sure to hear a message of a loving God who wants to be loved in return from a man who once had been lost beyond imagination, but now was showing others the way of hope.

There were about ten rows of pews on each side of the sanctuary setting the capacity of the church at about two hundred people, which was seldom achieved except during the once a year revivals that Joe would host. They were the solid, wooden kind with no padding whatsoever. Windows lined both sides of the main level, which was lit mostly by the natural stream of sunlight coming in through the clear-paned glass. The floors were also wooden with the exception of a carpet runner that went down the middle of the pews and some carpeting at the front and back of the church. There was the typical wooden information board mounted on the front wall that listed the page numbers of the hymns to be sung as well as the number in attendance from the prior week, which had climbed respectably since Reverend Huff had taken over. An acoustic piano flanked Joe to his left serving as the only means of instrumental music for worship.

There was no microphone to be found, nor was one needed. The rich voice that God had blessed Joe with and that he had honed over all his years of singing was completely sufficient to fill the little church at a level all could plainly hear and enjoy. When preaching, he had a natural ability of using his voice to inflect the proper tone and volume at just the right time based on the particular effect he was trying to make. If it was a message of comfort, he could speak in a soft, soothing manner as his baritone voice calmly vibrated sending the sounds floating ever so smoothly through the air. On the other hand, if he felt like a point needed to be firmly instilled in his audience, he could raise his voice and send the words violently echoing off the walls and ceiling in such a powerful and rich way that no one could escape hearing every last booming syllable.

Joe's singing voice made it possible for him to be the church's choir and song leader. On many Sundays he would also provide the special music. With little resources of their own to pull from, God had given the small congregation a powerful, dynamic preacher who, despite his advanced age, was a rock of a man with a heavenly voice, a piercing message and a heart bigger than the building in which he was serving.

To be around Joe on a Sunday was an absolute privilege. From the time he awoke in the morning until the final prayer of the service several hours later, the typical ornery and playful demeanor Joe usually displayed was purposefully absent. In its place was a focused intensity that can only be described as that of a boxer in the quiet moments before a raging title bout. It was his "game face" and there was nothing contrived or superficial about it. It was the result of a man who had full awareness of the serious nature and eternal significance of the duties he was preparing to carry out.

The hour-long car ride to church was quiet and peaceful, as Joe would be taking himself through his sermon in his mind along the way. It didn't matter to Joe that his "arena" wasn't the biggest or fanciest around. He didn't base the time and effort he invested on the number of people to whom he would be preaching. He treated each and every person in his church as the most important person in the world, which is exactly the way God views His creation.

Most Sundays after the service was over, Joe and Mary would spend the afternoon ministering to a widow of the church or someone who was ill and couldn't be there in person. Every life he could help bring into eternity was worth everything Joe had to give, and he gave it all every single time he had the chance to get up on that small platform and proclaim God's Word.

Joe's life was not a contradiction; his service was dedicated, consistent and powerful. He had entered the ring of service to God and he was not about to turn his back to Satan. God had prepared, armed and placed Joe where He wanted him to be and he had answered the bell at every round. There were still bouts to be fought, but the war had already been won and Joe knew it. Jesus had won the war against evil when He died on the cross at Calvary. Joe had to continue to fight with every ounce of courage and strength left in him. Just as he wouldn't stay on the sidelines when a game was going on in his front yard, he would not stay on the stool in the corner of the ring when God rang the bell for another round to begin.

The decade of the 70's seemed in direct contrast to Joe's life of service. It was marked with turmoil, social unrest and legal decisions in direct contradiction to what Joe believed. There were terrorist attacks and the Watergate break-in occurred, which led directly to the first presidential resignation in history, that of Richard M. Nixon. The fact that in the same decade abortion was made legal and test tube babies were born is evidence to the contradiction of life going on in this time. Society made it legal to end life, while still searching for ways to create it.

This decade was coming to an end, as was the time God had given Joe to serve. There were still things that had to be done, and Joe attacked each and every opportunity with full force. He had a few years left and still felt he had people who needed to be reached. There was retirement from Kernel's, but not retirement from God's work. Joe would not quit until he could no longer be God's servant. Until the final stage of the Seven Ages of Man descended, Joe would be in the ring punching away at Satan's evil schemes in the battle for souls.

CHAPTER EIGHT

The Eighth Decade
1980-1990
Age 70-80

"However, I consider my life worth nothing to me, if only I may finish the race and complete the task the Lord Jesus has given me-the task of testifying to the gospel of God's grace."
Acts 20:24

The decade of the 80's was ushered in by the phenomenon of the Rubik's Cube. For those who don't remember this device it was a cube with different colors on each side and those sides were moveable so that each line could be manipulated in multiple directions. The object was to mess up the cube and then get all colors back into the proper alignment. It was a mentally challenging task and few could get to the successful completion. It was at this same time that Joe and those around him began to notice a challenge for him mentally as well. Time had begun to take its toll on Joe and he began to forget things, began to speak less and listen more, and it was tougher and tougher for him to arrange the pieces of his life as he had been able to do before. To live his daily life became a challenge for Joe, he didn't need the challenge of the cube.

It was also early in 1980 that the concept of a book on his life came into being. Joe's son and his youngest daughter had gone into business together. On a trip to pick up goods for the business with his son-in-law they began to share stories of Joe's youth; specifically about his time in the Navy as they were passing through Chicago. At first reluctant, Joe agreed to do the tapes this book is based upon with stipulations; that no one would hear the tapes until after his death and that the book would not be started until then either. Both those stipulations were agreed to and honored. Over the next two years, Joe recorded the memories of his life in the quiet of his study. This was the same study where he had carefully prepared his sermons.

It is obvious after hearing the tapes that during this time God gave Joe the clarity of thought and purpose needed to produce them. The time Joe spent talking into the recorder was his preparation of the perpetual sermon contained in the message of salvation he desired this book to convey.

Early in this decade the first of the medical signs that his mind and body were shutting down occurred. On a pleasant, warm summer day in Central Indiana, Joe and Mary were sitting at the breakfast bar in their beloved country dream home they had built on the land next to the old home on Fairview Road. The couple had several traditions they had established in their retirement years and one was sitting down together for a light lunch. Each time it was the same. They fixed their meal, sat down together, prayed with each other, blessed the food and at the AMEN, they would lean toward each other, share a kiss and tell each other, "I love you." After nearly fifty years, the love and devotion for one another and their dedication to their faith grew with each passing day.

This day, however, did not go as others had. Shortly after the "I love you" had been shared, Joe suddenly looked at Mary with a sort of blind stare, would not respond to any verbal callings, and even though he never closed his eyes, became totally non-responsive. After a few short panicked seconds, Joe was helped to the floor and paramedics were called. By the time they arrived, Joe had come back to his senses, but this was the first, startling sign his physical body was beginning to fail. After that event, his mind was also never quite the same. The physical result of this first event was that a pacemaker was placed in Joe's chest. His body was failing, but his zeal for the Word of God and his desire to share it with the attendees at Freedom Christian

Church were still burning strong in the heart now paced electronically.

Joe's faithful service to his flock at Freedom Christian Church continued until 1982. He was continuing to get weaker and weaker physically as well as mentally, but it seemed God used Mary at this time to be Joe's strength. She began to do more and more of the household duties that Joe would have normally done, and she began to have to speak for him at times when she realized his mind wasn't working like it had in the past. What was amazing, however, was how the Holy Spirit would seem to just take over when Joe got behind the pulpit on a Sunday morning. Those he was serving had no idea he was having "spells", and when he got up on Sunday morning and got in his place with God, the Holy Spirit would take over and speak powerfully through the temple of God that time was slowly tearing down.

Finally on August 29, 1982 Joe and Mary knew it was time for him to leave the full-time pastorate position and let someone else fill the pulpit. It was not easy for Joe to finally come to the realization his full-time service had come to an end, but in his heart and mind he knew he could not serve at the level needed. So on a Sunday in late Summer at Freedom Christian Church, Joe preached his last sermon as a full-time minister of God. From his early years of protection through his years of forgiveness, God had brought Joe to his final years of service. There still exists a copy of that last sermon caught on tape. To listen, one would never have known it was delivered from the frail body and failing mind of a seventy-two year old man.

Joe's notes typed on his beloved Webster XL 500 show what his mission for the church was and continued to be for all those years he shepherded this small flock in west central Indiana. He first used 2 Timothy 4:2 which says;

> *"Preach the Word; be prepared in season and out of season; correct, rebuke and encourage-with great patience and careful instruction."*

He then went on to Psalm 6:8;

"Trust in Him at all times; ye people, pour out your heart before Him: God is a refuge for us." KJV

Without question, Joe had taught the truth to this congregation for all those years and it is evident from his last notes he wanted to be sure he left them with the same message he began with those thirteen years before. He used Proverbs 4:11 and 18 to drive home his point of what God had sent him there to do;

"I have taught thee in the way of wisdom; I have led thee in right paths. But the path of the just is as the shining light, that shineth more and more unto the perfect day." KJV

Joe went on that August day to preach the truth of the one and only way of salvation one last time. He used Acts 4:12 to focus the people he loved so much;

"Neither is there salvation in any other; for there is no other name under heaven given among men, whereby we must be saved." KJV

Joe's notes to himself under this scripture speak volumes of his passion to share with the unsaved. His words are as follows; "Salvation is what the Bible is all about. The main character is Jesus. As He said, 'I am the Way', salvation benefits are free, but many would rather pay the price to Satan."

Joe's last two points were, most assuredly, some of the hardest words he ever had to speak. He first used John 16:22;

"And ye now therefore have sorrow; but I will see you again, and your heart shall rejoice, and your joy no man taketh from you." KJV

The Eighth Decade

Under this point in his notes Joe wanted to make sure he conveyed the fact that even though he would not be there on a full time basis, he would still be "on call" for anyone who needed him, and he was.

His last point was underscored by scripture from the book of 2 Corinthians and written and spoken by one of Joe's favorite Biblical men, Paul. In 2 Corinthians 13:11 Paul speaks these words, which were the final words in Joe's sermon;

"Finally, brethren farewell, be perfect, be of good comfort, be of one mind, live in peace; and the God of love and peace shall be with you." KJV

There were few dry eyes in the church that day. All did not want to see Joe go. Many of Joe's family also attended the service and most understood now that this strong, vibrant man of God was slowly being taken away from them. His voice, sermon and delivery that day made all in the church understand that this final sermon was really the beginning of the end of a long life of service. Not because Joe or anyone else wanted it to be coming to an end, but just the pure fact of life that there is an ultimate end of time here on earth.

One should not believe at this point that Joe's service was totally complete. Joe was an ordinary man who God used in an extraordinary way. He continued to fight against the physical and mental struggles he was facing. He found ways to cope and conceal his loss of memory and he also went back to serving at his local church that meant so much to he and Mary. They began to attend Fairview Christian Church, just down the road from their house and both immediately got involved in teaching and serving. Joe also took over the job of church treasurer and served in that capacity for as long as he possibly could.

Even though time and illness began to take its toll on Joe through the next few years, he did not give up or go down easy. Joe fought to hang on to the way of life he had grown to love so much. His character and habits never really went away and in the beginning stages of his illness, he began to lean on Mary to compensate for the things he could no longer do. When put into a situation where his mind would fail him, he would give her a look that both seemed to understand. Mary realized he was in a place where he could not recall what was needed and she would carefully and lovingly fill in the blanks for him.

At this stage of life, his middle to late seventies, no one really ever gave a firm diagnosis of what was going on with Joe's physical and mental health. Those who did not know or understand could not see a quick or certain deterioration of Joe's condition. Those in the family, however, could see the decline. Not in the normal things, but the subtle changes were becoming more and more evident. Although he would still have his daily routine of cold coffee, preparing for the day, and his normal diet of cartoons, news and favorite TV, there were other events that gave clues of his losing the fight against time. In the past, when the ball game was taking place with the grandchildren in the front yard, Joe would be the first up to bat and running the bases. Now, he still would get out and be a part of the game, but he had to elicit the help of one of the younger kids to run once he had sent the ball toward the fence line between him and his neighbor. He still had the desire, but time had robbed him of the ability.

He also continued to bowl up until his 80th birthday, which had been one of his goals. Again, those with whom he had bowled all these years could really see no outward decline in Joe because he was a master of hiding his shortcomings. He would not speak rather than let someone know he couldn't answer a question or be a part of a conversation.

Even though he was slowly being robbed of his ability to communicate, he enjoyed his life and continued to serve. At selected times through the early 1980's he would still fill in on a temporary basis for pastors who were sick or on vacation. Joe had developed a reputation for his powerful preaching and his

The Eighth Decade

steadfast message of salvation through the acceptance of Jesus as Lord and Savior. And because he was able to compensate for his loss of memory, many did not know of the problems he was having. He renewed his service at the local nursing home and provided for those finishing their lives away from their homes and loved ones. There came a time too, however, that the advancing problems with memory and communication took this opportunity for service away as well.

Some men and women would give up, letting age and advancing disease control their life and slip peacefully into the good night, but not Joe. He continued to enjoy his life and those around him. Instead of complaining and feeling sorry for himself, he continued to do all he could to hold off the onslaught of the attacks to his mind and body. When the family would get together, he would still have the familiar gleam in his eye and head directly for the first grandchild through the door to pester and tease with them until Mary would finally yell, "George, leave those kids alone." He would then produce the impish smile all loved so much and go back to his brown leather recliner to bask in his joy until the next child arrived. This scene played out over again and again until all were safely in the house and had been adequately tormented by Grandpa Huff.

During the 1980's many significant events took place. The wreck of the Titanic was found after so many years of searching. Joe had lived through the sinking of the great vessel as well as through the discovery of the sunken remains. The wreck was much like Joe's life. The vessel of his earthly body was being destroyed slowly but surely just as the Titanic was being destroyed by the years of decay on the ocean floor. Unlike the Titanic however, Joe's life would continue for eternity and he had the promise of being raised to the heavens in perfection before God because he had accepted Jesus Christ as his Lord and Savior.

SECTION FOUR

Served

"This service that you perform is not only supplying the needs of God's people but it is also overflowing in many expressions of thanks to God."
2 Corinthians 9:12

CHAPTER NINE

The Ninth Decade

1990-1997
Age 80-87

"For I am already being poured out like a drink offering, and the time has come for my departure. I have fought the good fight, I have finished the race, I have kept the faith. Now there is in store for me the crown of righteous, which the Lord, the Judge, will award to me on that day-and not only to me, but also to all who have longed for his appearing."
2 Timothy 4:6-8

During the early years of 1990 through 1992 several different ideas were proposed regarding Joe's condition. The family was told he was suffering from dementia, mini-strokes and several other explanations for his constant and ever increasing slip into non-communication and inability to function. Finally in 1992, there was a definitive diagnosis from Methodist Hospital that Joe was suffering from Alzheimer's disease and there was no hope for any improvement in his condition. Although all had feelings that this was the case, the finality of the diagnosis still came with great emotional pain. To think of this proud, bright, athletic, talented man being systematically rendered helpless was more than anyone who knew him wanted to believe.

There were attempts at medication to stop the progress of the disease, but to no avail. Along with his decline mentally, there was also a corresponding decline in his physical body. Although not as rapid as the mental demise, the physical body was also succumbing to the years of earthly existence. Joe's arthritic knees made it more and more difficult for him to walk for any distance and do even the most simple of tasks. No longer could he make his walk out to the mailbox to bring in the mail or take out the garbage. The most difficult thing for him to give up was climbing on his lawnmower to care for his lawn. Having the need for someone else to serve him by doing this was a major turn of events.

As the Alzheimer's progressed and Joe became less and less able to communicate, some felt more comfortable talking about him instead of to him when he was in the room. For those who knew and loved Joe, they would try and get others to understand that even though Joe couldn't talk, that didn't mean he couldn't hear and understand.

The only way of describing what was evidently going on in Joe's life at this time is to say it was like he was trapped within his own body and couldn't get out. The Joe all knew and loved was still in there, but he just couldn't communicate in the old way. This concept of being trapped was evident through his eyes and his actions. The second example was when he was watching TV, especially boxing. You could still see him move with the punches of the fighters, but the movements weren't as crisp and the gleam in his eyes was beginning to fade. Those serving him at this stage of his life had to work just a bit harder to understand the meaning of his attempts to communicate.

A proud man who had just concluded years of service to others was now at a point in his life where he was becoming totally dependent on others to serve him. This was not an easy transition for Joe or anyone else who knew him. From being independent to now requiring others to do even the most simple of tasks for him was hard for Joe to tolerate. This could be seen again in his eyes and his actions even though by now he could no longer verbalize but a few words, and many times those words were just sounds as a child would make when beginning to learn to talk.

The time finally came when his beloved Mary could no longer take care of Joe in their home on Fairview Road. He could no longer make it to the bathroom by himself and could not walk without assistance. Even though his body had continued to deteriorate, he still was heavy enough that Mary could not lift or handle him. There were not many alternatives. As other families have had to face, something had to be done. All three children worked and had families, but no one wanted to see Joe have to go to a nursing home if at all possible. Billy finally decided that he would take Mary and Joe in with him and care for them. It was a most selfless act of service to the father and mother that had been so good to him. If possible all three children would have done the same thing, but Billy stepped up and took them into his home in Rushville, Indiana.

From the very beginning it was hard on everyone. Billy's family was disrupted, as was the normal life of Joe and Mary. Joe knew he wasn't in familiar surroundings and he continued to fail, not because those who loved him weren't serving in a most sacrificial way, but because the Alzheimer's was progressing at an accelerated rate. As a matter of fact, the willingness to serve displayed by Billy and his family at this juncture is indicative of the dedication and love throughout the entire Huff family structure. Much of this love and dedication is a result of the way Joe had loved and served the family through most of his life.

One evening it became apparent to all that something was very wrong with Joe physically. He could not verbalize what he was feeling, but it appeared to be something serious. The family took him to the hospital at Rushville and there the doctors began to try and diagnose the problem. At one point they felt they would have to operate because they found what they thought to be a mass in his lower abdomen. Again, Joe couldn't talk, so he couldn't help the doctors by explaining what he was feeling. After further investigation and tests, the doctors found that Joe had lost his ability to empty his bladder and once they placed a catheter, he was quickly relieved and the problem was alleviated.

Because of his advanced stage of Alzheimer's and his continuing physical condition, the doctors suggested that Joe stay in extended care at the hospital until he could be stabilized. This short stay at Rushville Extended Care was another example of

Joe's legacy in life. Every day he was there he had visits from children, grandchildren and friends. Joe was loved and respected by family and friends alike and their care and concern for him showed. Those he had served and loved for so many years were now returning those same acts to him in his time of need.

It is interesting to note and must be discussed that not all who were in positions of service were the examples of service Joe had been. For reasons only known to them, some who were there to care for Joe's needs seemed to be "put out" by this needy individual. Rather than having a heart and desire to serve the one less fortunate, they seemed to want to put his needs aside and tend to themselves instead of him. Surely the jobs of doctor, nurse, nurse's aid, and orderly are difficult at best, but still people in those positions can be ambassadors of comfort and care to the patient as well as the family. Yes, these folks didn't know the pre-Alzheimer's Joe, but by taking just a little time for caring and conversation, they could have easily gained the knowledge of the strong man of God he was.

One evening just before the decision was made to move Joe to another facility, one closer to he and Mary's home, it was as if God gave the family and Joe one last chance to communicate in a very meaningful and direct way. Joe was rapidly declining and seemed to be slipping away. Suddenly one evening he sat up in bed and began to speak in a logical, very understandable and concise manner. Everyone there was amazed and somewhat at a loss as to what was taking place. It lasted only for a short period that one evening, but it brought great joy and happiness to everyone. It was as if God was rewarding Joe and his family with one final good-bye.

It was just a short time later after much prayer, conversation and family meetings that it was decided to move Joe to a nursing home in Lebanon, Indiana. This would make it closer to home and allow Mary to move back into their home and attempt to regain some semblance of a normal life and let her get back to her church. This final move was emotional to say the least, and a bit ironic. This nursing home Joe was going to was the very same nursing home where he had, only years before, gone to minister to the residents. The place where he went to do his last acts of service would now be the very place he would last be served.

At the facility in Lebanon, he was initially placed alone in a room that contained two hospital-type beds. Joe occupied the one nearest the door in the sterile, sparsely furnished room. As is frequently the case when people enter the final stages of life, he required very few of his own belongings. A small closet-type area with a single shelf was in one corner of the room. The few articles Joe needed; his house slippers, some clothes and his dentures were kept there.

One of the symptoms that forced the move to the nursing home was the fact that Joe was having difficulty eating solid foods; he would tend to choke when trying to swallow. To help him through this, Mary would stop and pick up a chocolate milkshake for him every day before coming for her visit. The only other primary sustenance he would take was orange soda pop that the family would make sure was on-hand in ample supply.

The majority of the time in his early stages of being in the nursing home, Joe was cared for by a male nurse in his mid-forties. He seemed to be the only person on staff who had any success getting Joe to eat solid food. Although this man seemed to generally enjoy Joe, something happened one day that no one completely understands. Something caused Joe to become upset and no one else was in the room except the male nurse. Despite the rapid deterioration of mind and body, Joe became agitated to the point that he mustered up a tremendous amount of strength and struck the nurse with such force that the man was injured, requiring medical attention and subsequently missed several days of work. The outburst was in no way characteristic of Joe at the time. He had become very placid and did not show much energy any longer. Yet somehow, he still had the internal fight to, for whatever reason, express himself physically when he could no longer do so by any other means. Despite the short amount of time that he had been caring for Joe, the male nurse was quick to forgive the outburst and faithfully showed an interest in Joe's condition for the remainder of his stay.

Joe spoke very few words after being moved into the nursing home. Alzheimer's had built an invisible prison inside Joe separating his mind from his mouth. Instead of speaking, he communicated with facial expressions, gestures and most of all, his eyes. The voice that had characterized Joe all those many years was now nearly silenced. Such was his difficulty in communicating, that one day Joe's son-in-law arrived to hear loud guttural sounds emanating from the room. They weren't words, just loud sounds being made by forcing air strongly from the deep recesses of his throat. It was obvious Joe had been trying to get a message out, but no one seemed to be able to determine what he needed. Sensing he was just thirsty, the son-in-law got him a glass of orange drink and, not until two full glasses were completely emptied, did Joe once again show signs of contentment.

Because Joe couldn't speak for himself, the staff of the facility knew little about him and all the wonderful things his life represented. To help enlighten them to the life of this amazing man of God who was now in their care, Joe's family created a collage of pictures on a piece of poster board with captions underneath each one depicting who he was, and the things that had been important to him over the course of his life. There were pictures of him in an athletic context; one of Joe showing off the boxing gloves he had received for his birthday, and another of him playing in the yard with the grandchildren. There were pictures of him as husband, father and grandfather. And there were pictures of Joe, the pastor. The common theme of the collage was the vibrancy and love for life that Joe possessed and, most importantly, the love he had for others.

As the Christmas season of 1996 approached, the family

brought in a small tree to decorate Joe's room, and Mary kept him warm with a lap robe that she had crocheted with her own hands. At the beginning of January, the family held a small celebration of what was to be Joe's last birthday. God had sustained him long enough for this to take place in a private room. Shortly thereafter, Joe's condition had deteriorated to the point where the facility determined that physical therapy was no longer providing any benefit. As a result, Joe was moved to a larger room that he shared with three other men and his poster was brought along with him.

In his new location, Joe was next to a window in the bed furthest from the door. Despite his inability to say so, Joe immediately showed signs of not being comfortable in his new environment. He rarely got out of bed after being moved to the new room and most of the time laid there with his eyes closed. He wasn't sleeping all the time; it was just as if his disease had forced him deeper within the confines of his personal prison of silence.

The nursing staff suggested that a radio might be soothing for him, so one was brought in from his home. It seemed to help, but one Sunday afternoon his daughter came to visit and found the radio had been turned to a country station, which was not Joe's favorite kind of music. He lay there motionless with eyes opened only slightly and seemingly unfocused. His daughter reached over and turned the radio to a station that was broadcasting a church service. In a powerful display of the inner life still within, Joe immediately sat up in his bed and his eyes became brighter upon hearing the spiritual sounds now coming from the radio. He clenched his fists and started making motions with his arms showing his excited approval of the act of kindness his daughter had just done. The message of his actions was unmistakable. Joe was making it known that his passion for God was still burning bright and strong as ever inside his tired body.

On Thursday, February 20, 1997 Joe was moved for the last time in the nursing home. The family was called early in the day and was told they thought Joe's life was quickly coming to an end. The staff served the family and Joe well by moving him to a private room so there could be solace while they waited for the inevitable. On that same day, with many of his family members at his side, Joe's body succumbed to the disease that had taken hold of him and he passed away.

He had taken a lot of punches in his life both literal and figurative, but with God as the manager in his corner, Joe won the only title bout that matters in life. He had accepted Christ as his Savior and turned his heart over completely to the Lord. Now Joe's soul was at peace as he entered into the glorious presence of the Almighty.

During the first three decades of Joe's life God protected him through many tragic events and personal trials. The middle decades were characterized by God's matchless grace and forgiveness of Joe's sinful past as well as the gradual deepening and strengthening of his faith. Then, in an amazing testament to the fact that it's never too late to make a difference, the latter decades of Joe's life were filled with service to his fellow man under the guidance of his Heavenly Father, Joe's ultimate mentor and friend.

At the end of his life he could not speak, but years earlier the recordings Joe made captured his voice so it could endure beyond his years on this earth. Joe was extremely passionate about the message he conveyed on those tapes made in the sanctuary of his small study. It is only fitting that Joe have the opportunity, through the use of his words, to give the ending to this book:

> *...And for all the people, maybe some will understand, that God has a purpose for each and every one of us. There's a better way of life. There's a life to serve Him, a life that can answer all questions. Those who are searching need to search no more because He's just a prayer away. His loving kindness will fill the heart of any man no matter who he is, no matter where he's at, God will take care of him because God loves him. If God hadn't loved him,*

He wouldn't have sent his Son to die on Calvary for him. That is my prayer. That anybody within reach of any minister hearing any sermon preached, that their heart will fill with the love of God and His glory shall shine in their hearts forever. If we give our hearts to the Lord, give Him our love; He in turn will shower His love upon us. He will tend to our every need. We will never want, even though life seems rough and things go wrong. God never promised us a rose garden. We must suffer with the wicked also. We will have our trials and tribulations, but thank God He has a place for us where all these things shall pass away and we shall live in an eternity of love, of happiness and we shall never want again. So, in closing, I hope and pray that this has given you insight…What I want to do is impress upon others' lives the life that I lived and the life that I now live and God has made it all possible. So I thank Him as I pray in His precious name that He will help others as He has helped me. And to Him be the praise and the glory forever. Amen.

Post Script

Joe's life is an example for anyone who is searching for the "truth" about life as well as those who have already found Jesus as their personal Lord and Savior. The book is written as a legacy for Joe and as a gift to his family, especially to his faithful wife Mary. It comes with the prayer that his life will continue to speak to and change hearts just as he has already done for so many others. To have Joe's own words on audio tape is truly a gift from God and offered the opportunity for him to personally assist in the writing of this book.

There were so many events and memories on the tapes that all could not be included in this book, but one portion of the recordings must be given to the reader at this time, otherwise Joe's message would not be complete. The following is a poem that he reads on the tapes two different times. The tone of his words, the emotion in his voice and the fact he repeated the poem suggests a sense of urgency that he wanted each of us to take to heart the message it contains:

Regret

I bow my head in sorrow,
My eyes they fill with tears
When I look back across my life
And see the wasted years.

Down through the years I wandered
Without a goal in mind
Until at last He found me,
My Savior good and kind.

He left his realm of glory,
Of heaven far above
And came to die on Calvary
To prove His gracious love.

God knows that I am sorry
And He's forgiven me,
But how I wish the wasted years
Were given back to me.

That I might live each one again
In service for my King
And for the wealth He's given me
Some small gift I could bring.

Andrew Murray

The last sermon Joe preached was attended by many people and by most of his family. Looking back at that day little did most realize how his message was God inspired and directed to be reflected on again and again by all who heard it that day as well as all who will read this book.

His central message was what it always was, the need for the acceptance of the Lord Jesus Christ as personal Savior in order to enter the gates of Heaven. But this day Joe had a renewed vitality and fervor for what he was saying to those who would hear and those words will continue to resonate through all who hear them for years to come.

The authors of this book would like to end this attempt at capturing the life of one we loved so much with the scripture he used in his last public ministry to leave with the congregation who had become his friends.

"Finally, brothers, good-bye. Aim for perfection, listen to my appeal, be of one mind, live in peace. And the God of love and peace will be with you." 2 Corinthians 13:11